You Can't Be Serious!

Mike Kerr

You Can't Be Serious!

Putting Humor to Work

MICHAEL KERR

Front cover photograph: Claudine Dumais
Back cover photograph: Claudine Dumais
Illustrations by Bill Leinweber
Covers and interior design by Articulate Eye Design, Saskatoon, Saskatchewan

Printed in Canada

CANADIAN CATALOGUING IN PUBLICATION DATA

Kerr, Michael, 1962 –
    You can't be serious!

    ISBN 0-9688461-0-6

Humor in the workplace. I Title.
  HF5549.H85K47 2001   658.3'14   C2001-910197-X

Speaking of Ideas. . .
322 Canyon Close,
Canmore, Alberta,
T1W 1H4
1-866-609-2640

TABLE OF CONTENTS

— ACKNOWLEDGEMENTS —

Numerous folks generously offered their help, stories, cookies, ideas and jokes to help bring this book together. Some helped without even knowing it, while others helped out without even being asked to.

I'd like to express my most heartfelt thanks to each and every-one of the following: Rhonda Allen, Sherry Auger, Dr. Gordon Chin, Todd Defrancesca (a.k.a. absoluttodd), Doug Driediger, Nadine Fletcher, Joel Hagen, David Huggill, Larry Halverson, David Kerr, David Levin, Marceline O'Connor Johnson, Steve Kutanzi, Dr. Diana Mahony, Courtney Page (#17), Robert Throckmorton (The Flying Buttress) and Steve Wilson from the World Laughter Tour.

Brian Patton was always available to share invaluable and wacky insights over a cup of coffee. Geri Rowlat did a masterful job editing the final text. And a huge thank you once again to Mike McCoy and Brian Smith from Articulate Eye Design, for their com-bined wizardry in designing another great looking book and cover (of course, considering the cover model they had to work with, how could they have gone wrong?).

A special thanks to Bill Leinweber for coming through at the 11th hour with his wonderful work on the cartoons.

Finally, thanks to Claudine Dumais for her constant support and reminding me more than once to take my own advice and laugh once in a while.

— *FOREWORD* —

When I was ten (years, not pounds) I was asked to stay after school with three other aspiring criminals. I forget what heinous felony we committed, but I do recall the punishment. We were forced to stand straight as beanpoles in a row and remain perfectly still, like well-behaved pups. Within two minutes, something deep inside me screamed to be let out. And no, it wasn't gas.

Trying to fight off a giggle fit is like trying to stuff Jello into a sock. You just can't do it, at least not without creating a mess. It's especially difficult to do with a teacher glaring at you, telling you to be quiet. And to be still. And to take this seriously. The more she scowled, the harder the laugh-demons inside me fought to be freed.

By the five-minute mark, the four of us were on the verge of contracting a roaring case of deliciously contagious and deliriously infectious giggles. But, before our giggles threatened to boil over into outright laughter, I (having been designated as the ring leader) was hauled down to the principal's office by the teacher. I then had to sit perfectly still while I endured a lecture about the error of my giggling ways and on the importance of taking things seriously. I left school that day wondering what was wrong with a little laughter in the world. And surely, I hoped, all adults couldn't be such grumps when it came to laughter.

Now that I'm older and wiser (but no less prone to a good giggling fit), I have the answer. Not all adults take things too seriously - just most of them. Or at least, far too many of them.

Of course, as we grow up we learn what a serious place the adult world is – there's war, disease, poverty, pollution, crime and death. And in our business lives there's serious stuff going on there, too – mergers, profit margins, hostile takeovers and bottom lines. No wonder adults are so darned serious.

So I've decided, for better or worse, for richer or poorer, that one of my missions in life will be to convince some of the perpetually serious business folks out there to *lighten up* before they *crack up*. It's not an easy job, but someone's got to do it.

So what are my qualifications for this task? Well, I certainly didn't study humor in university (but you *can* now). I studied forestry, not a field known for its humor, although the terms "buttress" and "root rot" always made me laugh. My serious study of humor actually began when I lost my sense of humor. I looked for it everywhere. I took out ads in the paper, called the police, and put posters up at laundromats. I stopped strangers on the street and asked if they'd seen it. After three months of exhaustive searching, I was still without my sense of humor.

But I wasn't alone. Some co-workers had lost theirs too. It was watching the heart, humanity and humor being sucked out of our workplace faster than you can say "Dilbert has left the office" that made me ponder this "humor in the workplace" thing. And finally I decided to do something about it. I attended an international humor conference. I devoured hundreds of books, scientific papers and magazine articles relating to humor and workplace culture. Then I interviewed countless numbers of people in countless numbers of businesses. And before long, I realized that humor in the workplace is something that should, ironically, be taken *seriously*.

Over the years, I have become passionate about the topic for two main reasons. First, our work is how we have chosen to make our way through this amazing journey called life. It is, quite literally, how we go about *making* a life for ourselves. So we owe it to ourselves to make this thing called work an exciting, motivating, humanizing, heart-filled experience. Second, when we access our sense of humor, I think we are really accessing our humanity. Celebrating and sharing our humor are about being human, being authentic and being true to yourself.

This may sound a tad preachy, like I'm on my high humor horse, but I want you to know why I wrote this book. And above all else, I want to show you that I am serious about *not* being serious. Seriously.

Humor in the Workplace? You Can't Be Serious!

The one serious conviction that a man should have is that nothing is to be taken too seriously.
Samuel Butler

Humor in the workplace is the Rodney Dangerfield of human resources management. Like the tie-tugging, fidgeting comedian, the topic just doesn't seem to get any respect. In fact, when I suggest that people should add copious amounts of humor to their work lives, many people react with disbelief. "You want us to *what*? Make work more fun? Lighten up on the job? Mix business with pleasure? But, work isn't *supposed* to be fun," these indignant folks respond. "That's why we call it work, in fact, that's why work is a four-letter word! And you want us to add humor to our work lives? Surely, YOU CAN'T BE SERIOUS?"

And when these folks tell me, "You can't be serious!" about the idea of putting humor to work, I cleverly respond with, "You are absolutely right—you *can't* be serious!" In fact, that's the entire point of this book. You simply can't afford to be chronically serious in the workplace, at least not if you're interested in living a healthier, more sane and balanced life. And you can't be serious if you want to improve morale, motivate yourself or your employees, spark creativity, facilitate open communication, deliver more effective presentations, build trust between management and staff, offer memorable customer service and improve productivity in the workplace. There's no way you can be serious if you want to recruit top-notch employees, retain your best staff and reduce employee absenteeism rates. And if you want to manage stress more effectively, then you really can't be serious! You *can't* be serious because our sense of humor is one of our most undervalued, under-appreciated and underutilized human resources.

If you still have serious doubts about the value of humor in the workplace, I hope to change your mind long before you reach the end of the book. In the meantime, here's a summary of some compelling reasons to invest in humor, add more fun to your workplace and why, above all else, sometimes, you just *can't* be serious!

Laughter is the Best Medicine. It's a cliché because it's true. A good laugh reduces blood pressure, increases our heart rate, massages our internal organs and reduces serum cortical (a hormone released in response to stress). People who have a positive, healthy sense of humor may, according to some researchers, get sick less often and recover more quickly from illnesses. So if you want to live a healthier life, or if you want to have healthy employees and reduce absenteeism rates, then you can't be serious!

Humor Keeps You Balanced. Juggling personal goals, family commitments and work demands has never been more challenging. A recent *Fast Company* magazine survey reported that 91% of respondents said making their personal lives a bigger priority was "very important" to them. A healthy sense of humor is one of the most effective ways to keep grounded and balanced. After all, if *you're* not balanced, it's virtually impossible to keep all those balls in the air for long. And when you stumble or fumble, your sense of humor helps you maintain your sanity and perspective. So if you want to stay balanced, you can't be serious!

Laughter is a Powerful Stress Buster. Many psychologists tell us that humor is the complete opposite of stress. Humor reduces tension in a stressful situation, provides a realistic perspective when you most need it, gives you control over your emotions and helps you rise above a crisis. Humor is a thinking response in an emotional situation, helping you connect your mind with your heart. So if you want to manage stress better, you just can't be serious!

Humor is a Catalyst for Creativity. Humor and creativity are about looking at the same thing as everyone else and seeing something completely different. Both involve taking risks, playing with ideas and making new and often unlikely associations. Is it any wonder, then, that humor is one of the most effective catalysts for creativity in the workplace? Clearly, if you want to be more creative or to foster a more innovative work environment, you can't be serious!

Humor Helps Us Manage Change. For the 99.4% of you who are wrestling with major changes in the workplace, humor can go a long way towards making change less frightening and stressful. Humor encourages creative thinking and flexible attitudes, two key traits you'll find in people who manage change effectively. So if you want to master change in your work life, you can't be serious!

Humor is a Powerful Motivator and Morale Booster. Humor in the workplace keeps the mood light and maintains a climate of positive energy where morale is high. And when morale is high, co-workers get along better, people actually *want* to show up to work and employees are more committed to their goals. So if you want to fire up the troops (including yourself) and boost morale, you *really, really* can't be serious!

Humor is a Great Way to Say "Thanks!" Successful organizations celebrate every milestone on their journey to loftier goals; they know that's the key to long-term success. That's why many companies use creative, fun and even downright wacky ways to reward employees for a job well done and to say "thanks" for a great effort. If you want to reward accomplishments and employees effectively, then you can't be serious!

Humor Builds Strong Teams. Teams that laugh together work well together. Humor breaks down stereotypes and promotes a sense of unity in any workforce. It builds company traditions and a sense of shared history that reminds employees they are playing for the same team. So if you want to build a great sense of camaraderie in your workplace, then you can't be serious!

Humor Can Make Meetings More Effective. Humor in meetings encourages participation, minimizes conflicts, helps people retain information, opens up dialogue and sparks creativity. So if you catch yourself saying, "We've *got* to stop meeting like this," after every meeting, then you can't be serious!

Humor Facilitates Open Communication. Humor is a powerful way to connect at a human level and build rapport. It breaks down barriers and opens up hearts, creating an environment conducive to open, honest communication. Humor can also liven up dry business correspondence, soften authoritative messages and improve the delivery of business presentations. If you want to improve your communications, you can't be serious!

Humor Improves Customer Service. If you've got customers, then you're in the people business and, above all else, the relationship business. Including customers in the fun is an effective way to connect with clients, retain a loyal customer base and provide memorable customer service. If you are serious about providing outstanding customer service, then sometimes you can't be serious!

Humor Helps Managers Manage with a Lighter Touch. More and more business leaders are embracing their sense of humor as a way to build rapport with staff, communicate more effectively, show their human side more openly, develop trust and foster a supportive workplace climate. So if you want to be a more effective manager, then you can't be serious!

Laughter Can Improve the Bottom Line. If humor helps us achieve all the goals listed so far, then it only makes sense that ultimately it will improve our overall effectiveness and productivity in the workplace. This isn't, as hockey commentator Don Cherry would say, "rocket surgery." We do best what we enjoy doing. In fact, there are countless examples of businesses that, by focusing on their employees' laugh lines, have significantly improved their bottom lines. So if you want to be more successful and productive, then really, you can't be serious!

Humor Improves the Coffee in Your Office. Well, okay, I'm stretching it here (the truth is, I didn't want to leave the list at 13 - I mean no one makes a list with 13 points). But you know, there probably is a little truth to this statement. There's evidence that humor increases our tolerance for pain, so if your coffee is *really* bad, a little laughter might actually ease any ill side effects from rot-gut java. And, let's face it, when you're laughing a lot, having fun and enjoying work, isn't the coffee bound to taste a *little* better? Of course it is. Case closed. If you want to enjoy your coffee more, you just can't be serious! (*Are you sensing a recurring theme here?*)

FINAL THOUGHTS

There is one last compelling argument for adding more fun to our work lives. Life is simply too short. Yes, it's a cliché, yes, it's corny and yes, it stinks to high heaven of saccharine, but it's true! You don't hear a lot of people saying, "Boy this life thing sure is dragging, isn't it?" or "I'm only turning 50 today? Gee, I sure wish time would go faster!"

And since we're onto clichés, let's touch on another big one. When we're on our death beds, I'm quite certain most of us won't reflect back on our lives and think, "You know, I wish I'd been a more miserable s.o.b. at work," or "Boy, if I had to do it all over, I'd try to be more somber and scowl a lot more." In our golden years (but hopefully sooner), most of us will have figured out that the real bottom line in life has nothing to do with dollars, profits or stock options.

Life really *is* short. And whether we like it or not, our work has a huge impact on our lives. More than two-thirds of our waking hours (about 88,000 hours over a typical lifetime) are spent working. We often live in the communities where our work takes us. Many of our personal friendships develop out of working relationships (by one account, 50% of marriages result from meetings on the job). Our work helps define us, shape our personalities and nourish our growth as fully functional human beings. A large part of our self-esteem and identity is wrapped up in what we do for a living. For better or for worse, our work has a profound impact on the quality of our lives. Mihaly Csikszentmihalyi, author of *Flow—The Psychology of Optimal Experience*, goes further, suggesting that the two most important factors in determining our overall happiness are our relations with other people and how we experience our work. Additionally, some health researchers have found that work satisfaction is a better predictor of our future health than most other health-related habits. In other words, it makes a ridiculously monumental amount of sense to think about and, more importantly, *plan* to improve the quality of our work lives by putting humor to work each and every day.

So, if a serious person with an overly serious scowl walks up to you in the hallway, remind them of Oscar Wilde's wonderful words, "Life is too important to be taken seriously!" Then tell them, "You *can't* be serious!"

> *We need to stop looking at work as simply a means*
> *of earning a living and start realizing it is one of*
> *the elemental ingredients in making a life.*
>
> Luci Swindoll

— 1 —

Putting Humor in Its Place

People will readily admit that they have poor hand-writing, are poor at math or are a klutz. But they'll never admit they have a poor sense of humor.
— George Carlin

A survey of people just like you (not having met you, I can only assume they are just like you) suggests that 86% of people believe they possess an above-average sense of humor (*if you have a rudimentary grasp of math then you know 36% of these people are lying*). But what does it mean exactly, to have a sense of humor, let alone an above-average one? Does *everyone* have a sense of humor?

To further complicate things, when we try to put humor to work in the workplace, some people get downright nervous. So let's begin our journey into the world of workplace humor by clearing up some myths that people have about humor, and in particular the idea of humor in the workplace.

Myth #1: "I'm humorously challenged. I'm just not funny and I couldn't tell a joke if my life depended on it, so this topic doesn't really apply to me."

Surveys, including my own surveys of audiences I've spoken to, suggest that less than 5% of people believe they are good joke tellers. The other 95% are presumably like the rest of us—we either *begin* with the punchline or forget the punchline all together. Fortunately, the joke manglers of the world needn't despair. Having a good sense of humor has *nothing* to do with being able to tell a joke or even about being funny. *Psychology Today* reported the results of a study by Robert R. Provine, MD, which found that only 10 to 20% of laughter is preceded by jokes. So relax! When I recommend adding more humor to our work lives, I'm not suggesting we stand around the water cooler smoking a fat cigar sharing one-liners all day.

Having a sense of humor is about having a sense of balance, perspective and proportion. A sense of humor is the ability to recognize the incongruities and absurdities that confront us on a daily basis. In other words, it is the ability to look at the same thing as everyone else and see something just a little different. It's rather fitting that we call it a "sense" of humor because, as with our other senses, it is a way of taking in and processing information about the world around us.

To say that someone has a great sense of humor simply means that person can find the humor in a given situation. If your humor sense is finely focused for 20-20 humor vision, when you see a newspaper headline that reads "Stolen Painting Found By Tree," you'll think, "Wow, what a clever tree!" And when you see a sign in a fast-food restaurant proclaiming "We don't just serve burgers, we serve people!" you'll likely chuckle and say to yourself, "I wonder what people taste like?" And if complete chaos greets you on a Monday morning at the office, that same sense of humor helps you find *something* to laugh at in the midst of the mayhem.

Having a keen sense of humor is much more than just finding the humor in a situation, though. A well-developed humor sense helps you maintain your head in a crisis, problem solve in a creative fashion and manage your stress so that you can deal with problems head on. The ability to access your humor *really* is an important resource you can depend on in times of trouble. Having a sense of humor, then, isn't about *being* funny, it's about rolling with the punches, flowing with the current and letting the small things in life bounce harmlessly off you. It's about gaining control, not necessarily over what's happening to you, but at least over your emotions and reactions to it.

Our humor resource is also one of our most human characteristics; it differentiates us from weasels, snakes and sharks. So when we talk about bringing more humor into the workplace, we're really talking about *humanizing* the workplace—making it a place where humans (as opposed to weasels, snakes or sharks) actually want to spend time and perform at their highest potential.

And finally, one last question related to this myth: Does *everyone* really have a sense of humor? I think so (yes, *even* some of my former bosses and schoolteachers). Although genetics obviously plays a role in determining our personality, I don't for a moment believe that some of us are born with the HA HA gene, while others somehow missed out. Even Robin Williams admits to having been a painfully shy child growing up. Unfortunately some people bury their sense of humor deep inside themselves, and therefore have trouble *accessing* it. Our sense of humor is part skill, part attitude, and to a very large degree, a *learned* characteristic. Like any other skill or attitude, we can practice using our sense of humor and learn to develop, nurture and access it when we need it the most.

> *A sense of humor is maturity and wisdom; and there is no maturity and wisdom without a sense of humor.*
>
> — George Mikes

When was the Last Time You Wagged Your Tail?

Lenore Terre, author of BEYOND LOVE AND WORK: WHY ADULTS NEED TO PLAY, suggests that play teaches many animals to "get along in groups, traverse their terrain, master their bodies and to be more flexible." Many biologists believe that the ability of animals to play in **adulthood** is a sign of superior intelligence and that the level of play in animals increases with increasing complexity of the brain. Wolves, dolphins and monkeys, for example, all highly intelligent and socially evolved species, play a great ➤

deal as adults. Captive dolphins seem to enjoy splashing their trainers. Monkeys play hide and seek. And when wolf packs howl, there's always lots of excitement and play. Wolves wag their tails, lick each other's faces, play tug-of-war with sticks and generally have what appears to be a darn good time. So if you want to demonstrate your superior intelligence and social development, maybe **you** should howl and wag your tail a little more often!

> *What is the right way to live?*
> *Life should be lived as play.*
> — Plato

Myth #2: Don't worry, be happy . . . and all our problems will magically disappear!

> The Guru Baba Meher died in 1969; however, his last spoken words were uttered in 1925 before undertaking a lifelong vow of silence. His last words were: "Don't worry, be happy."

Some people believe that when the going gets tough, you simply grin from ear to ear, pat people on the back and tell everyone to turn their frown upside down. Do that long enough, they'll tell you, and your problems will vanish before your eyes. If only it was that simple.

Using humor to mask or avoid a potential problem helps no one. Some psychologists believe that people who sleepwalk their way through life with grins permanently etched on their faces tend not to have a well-developed sense of humor and don't manage stress effectively. Using humor as a shield is just as out of balance as wallowing in pity and not accessing your sense of humor at all. Rather than using humor to *avoid* dealing with issues, people need to develop a style of humor that helps them confront their problems.

Humor is not, and never will be, a blanket solution to all your workplace woes. Trying to introduce copious amounts of humor into a dysfunctional work environment with a high level of mistrust may even backfire, if not done carefully. Staff might view this newfound humor craze with cynicism, believing it's nothing more than the latest management fad someone read about in a respected, best-selling book (like this one). Worse still, staff may view it as an attempt by managers to cover up the fact that more serious problems exist.

Now having said all that, adding positive humor can *never* make a situation worse, even in a workplace where more serious issues lie beneath the surface. If you're going through a crisis, humor *will* help people to better manage change, deal with their stress and be more open and flexible—attributes you'll need to solve those deeper workplace issues. So rather than treating humor in the workplace like window dressing, use it as *part* of a comprehensive approach to managing people and fostering a more productive, healthy and creative work environment.

> *It is my belief, you cannot deal with the most serious things in the world unless you understand the most amusing.*
> — Winston Churchill

Checked Your Bodily Fluid Level Lately?

The term "humor" once referred to bodily fluids. Ancient Greeks believed that bodily humors (fluids) determined our moods. Angry people had too much bile in their system, while calm people had too much phlegm. They were right about one thing: our humor does lie deep inside us—inside our soul, spirit, heart and mind (I'm just not so sure it comes in liquid form, at least, not yet).

"You're down a quart of humor."

Myth #3: "I'm a professional, and if I have fun, people aren't going to think I take my job seriously!"

We've all met people who suffer from professionalitis. They're the people who went to school longer than the rest of us, who have 14 letters following their names (as in Joe Schmenko, B.A., MD, Ed., PhD, H2O, Y2K), who possess an important sounding title (like Assistant Director of the Adjudicator for Administrative Protocol, Procurement and Management) and, yes, who carry a briefcase. The briefcase, permanent scowl and zombie-like walk are all sure-fire signs that these folks are *professionals*. You can spot them a mile away. They might as well be carrying a neon sign flashing **Here Goes a Professional** above their head. These folks believe that they must take everything around them, especially themselves, seriously at all times, since to do otherwise is simply unprofessional. They worry that if they are seen smiling, laughing or, God forbid, having fun, they'll be accused of not taking their jobs seriously. Fortunately this condition is treatable, especially if detected in its earliest stages.

The treatment is painless and simple: it's learning to tell the difference between taking yourself seriously and your work seriously. One is necessary, the other is lethal. We need to believe in what we are doing and to take our work or mission in life as a serious undertaking, but that doesn't mean taking *ourselves* seriously. In fact, considering all the tremendous benefits of humor, we *need* to take ourselves lightly in *order* to be professional.

Some of the most outlandish examples of humor in the workplace come from professions that *really* do deal with life-and-death situations. Many doctors and nurses know the value of maintaining a well-balanced sense of humor. Often, the humor they use is known as "gallows humor" and, to an outsider, may not always be appreciated or understood. Yet the professionals on the inside of this stressful world depend on this humor to keep their sanity and distance themselves from the tragedy around them, so that they can perform their jobs as professionally as possible.

So if you take your job seriously, practice taking yourself lightly. And if you detect some early symptoms of professionalitis, recall the words of comedian George Carlin: "We're all amateurs. It's just that some of us are more professional at it than others."

I never did a day of work in my life—it was all fun!
— Thomas Edison

Wanted: Professional. Must Have Good Sense of Humor

Surveys tell us that upwards of 98% of CEOs would rather hire someone with a sense of humor than someone who is somber. Moreover, 62% of business school deans believe that humor and success are strongly related. And a California State University study revealed that when people have more fun on their job, they perform better. Even NASA recently suggested that when recruiting astronauts, one of the key traits they look for is a healthy sense of humor (imagine traveling all the way to Mars with a grump). So perhaps the time has come to consider some fitness training for **your** funny bone?

Give me the man who has enough
brains to make a fool of himself.
— Robert Louis Stevenson

Myth #4: "If I put out the humor welcome mat, employees are going to use it as an excuse to act childish and as a license to goof off."

"I can see it now," some managers moan. "There will be whoopee cushions at the next board meeting, executives dressing up like Elvis and streakers at our summer barbecue. Our office will become total anarchy! No work will ever get done and I just know someone is going to make me dress up like a chicken!"

Relax. *You Can't Be Serious!* is about using humor in a safe, relevant and appropriate manner. It's also about blending humor with our existing goals to help everyone become *more* efficient and productive, not less. I'm suggesting we need to be more *child-like* (curious, playful, creative, imaginative) on our jobs, not *childish* (so the chances of being forced to dress up like a chicken are slim, at best). And although there are a lot of positive benefits to "goofing off" in this over-caffeinated, hyperactive society, I'm not suggesting that humor or play be used as an excuse for chronic lollygagging about. Even in playful, humor-filled organizations, people are still held accountable. Indeed, there are numerous reasons why employees don't perform their jobs effectively that have *nothing* to do with a high level of fun in a work environment.

- ☂ Management hires the wrong people.
- ☂ Employees haven't been given clear goals or directions.
- ☂ Employees haven't been trained or given the proper tools.
- ☂ Talented people are wasted when the right people are given the wrong task to perform (known as "trying to turn an acorn into an elm" syndrome).
- ☂ Employees haven't been evaluated since the disco era.

Never, however, have I yet to find a single example of people who didn't perform their work proficiently because they were *enjoying what they were doing and having a great time doing it!*

> *When work is a pleasure, life is joy! When work is a duty, life is slavery.*
> — Maxim Gorky

Does **Your** Organization Have a Sense of Humor?

We usually attach personality traits to people, but is it possible for organizations to have a sense of humor? Absolutely. Like people, organizations have personalities that reflect their culture through their image, advertising, customer service, style of communication and how they treat their employees. Southwest Airlines, WestJet or Ben and Jerry's Ice Cream are companies that all convey a healthy sense of humor. So the question of the day is this: Does **your** company have a good sense of humor or does it take itself a little **too** seriously?

Why Do We Laugh?

For centuries people have pondered the questions: What causes laughter? Why do we laugh at certain things? Several theories have been put forth over the years, all explained in-depth in John Morreall's book, TAKING LAUGHTER SERIOUSLY. The superiority theory suggests we laugh when we feel superior over a situation or another person. The incongruity theory proposes we laugh at things that give us an unexpected, but pleasurable surprise. The relief theory suggests we laugh as a release of built-up, often nervous, energy. Morreall offers yet another alternative theory that borrows elements of these three and is summed up as follows: "Laughter results from a pleasant psychological shift." Perhaps what's more important than knowing **why** we laugh, is simply making sure we **remember** to laugh on a regular basis.

Time spent laughing is time spent with the Gods.
— Japanese proverb

Myth #5: The bottom line is the bottom line!

After my humor seminars, some managers approach me with a look of grave concern (you can practice this look—just furrow your brow, squint a little and lose the smile). They haven't quite bought into this whole "adding humor to work thing" because, as they remind me, in the world of business, the bottom line is profits, dollars and productivity. One business giant even shared with me, in a rather hushed toned, the following little gem, "The bottom line *is* the bottom line." (A brief confession—I used to think the bottom line was that little underwear line you see on people's bums.) These bottom-liners (not to be confused with bottom-feeders) are concerned that if they mix fun with business, their much-coveted bottom line will begin to sag. It's a concern that just doesn't hold water.

If putting humor to work in the workplace reduces stress levels, increases creativity, improves morale, strengthens teamwork, facilitates open communication, builds trust between management and employees and reduces employee absenteeism and turnover rates, then will it not ultimately lead to increased productivity? Of course it will. We do best what we enjoy doing. It's just that simple. Humor in the workplace is a means to a better end, not the end itself.

"We did not plan to build a billion-dollar company—just to have fun," says Jozef Straus, president of JDS Uniphase Corp., in a *Globe and Mail* interview. It's amazing how often similar thoughts are echoed by wildly successful people. This notion holds true in the world of sales. The top 5% of salespeople have one thing in common—they love what they do.

Binney and Smith, the makers of Crayola Crayons, cited an increase in sales from $92 million to $240 million between 1984 and 1990. One of the reasons cited for the jump in sales? They made the workplace more fun. Employees of Southwest Airlines, from CEO Herb Kelleher to the frontline staff, are known for their positive and playful attitudes on the job. In fact, the airline won a "humor in the workplace" award for its use of humor, and even hires for a sense of humor when recruiting new employees. Clearly, employees and customers have a lot of fun at Southwest Airlines, but the question asked by our bottom-liners is, "Are they successful?" Absolutely. Year after year, Southwest finishes first or near the top of the competition in nearly every measurable category in the airline industry, including customer satisfaction and productivity.

These examples are merely the tip of the iceberg. The bottom line is this: when it comes to the bottom line, a little laughter goes a long way.

> *The number one premise of business is that it need not be boring or dull. It ought to be fun. If it's not fun, you're wasting your life.*
> — Tom Peters, management expert

Myth #6: We're spoiled! All work and no play is the way it has always been.

There is a common misconception that primitive cultures spent most of their time barely eking out an existence. Life for these people was typically assumed to fall nicely under the "all work and no play" billing. Reality suggests that the opposite is true. Historically, primitive tribes spent a very small portion of time working. Early African and Australian tribes typically spent only 3 to 5 hours a day working; the remainder of the day was spent on rest and play. Mihaly Csikszentmihalyi, author of *Flow – The Psychology of Optimal Experience*, tells us that play and culture occupy more time than work in most primitive cultures. Other researchers discovered that the !Kung bushmen of the southwest Kalahari work only two and a half days a week to survive; about two-thirds of their time is spent visiting or entertaining visitors. A tribe in New Guinea spends more time looking for colorful feathers than working. One has to wonder, then, as a society, what progress we truly are making in our overworked and underplayed culture.

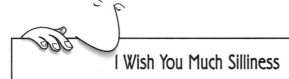

I Wish You Much Silliness

One of the many symptoms of professionalitis, or what I like to call **acute recurring adultness**, is the notion that silliness has no place in business or, for that matter, in adulthood. Considering the origin of the term "silly", however, we should perhaps rethink this. Silly is derived from the old English **saelig**, which meant "to be completely happy and blessed." Silly was a blessing you wished upon those you loved "to be happy, healthy and prosperous." So please, for you and your loved ones, I wish you nothing but a life full of silliness.

Myth #7: Humor is trivial.

> *Humor, I think, is responsible for more important human advances than physics, medicine or any other science. It teaches us to see things in proportion.*
> — George Mikes, humor author

"Okay, so maybe I can buy the fact that humor is useful. But can it really do *that* much for us? Isn't it just icing on the cake—it's nice to have, everyone likes it, but surely we can live without it?"

Sure. We could survive without humor in the workplace if we had to. We could also sleepwalk our way through life and count the years we have left until retirement. And our business can cruise along on autopilot, year after year. Sigh.

Or we could imagine another scenario, where we are fully awake and participating actively and completely in our work lives. Our workplaces are exciting, dynamic, creative and fully energized places to work. We can soar to new heights and achieve the kind of success we once only dreamed about. And we can become the kind of place where everyone wants to work.

Many organizations spend profuse amounts of time and money focused on their physical assets and "hard" skills, like budgeting and project management, while relegating topics like humor in the workplace to the "soft" side of the business ledger. But as business management author Tom Peters reminds us, focusing solely on profits is like trying to play tennis while watching the scoreboard. More and more leaders now recognize the so-called "soft stuff" is not trivial, indeed, it's the soft stuff, including humor in the work-place, that is *essential* to the success of any organization.

And, to counter the notion that humor is trivial, there are count-less tales of adventurers, explorers, hostages, cancer patients, nat-ural disaster victims and even holocaust survivors that pay tribute to the role played by their sense of humor in literally *saving their lives*. In his book *Man's Search for Meaning*, Viktor Frankl describes the horrific ordeal of surviving an internment camp during World War II. He had everything taken from him: his family, his profes-sion, his possessions and his home. The one thing Frankl vowed that no one could take away was his inner spirit and his sense of humor. He made a pact with a friend in the camp that each day they would share a joke or a humorous observation about life in the camp or about life after they were freed. For example, Frankl quipped about one of the camp guards, "Imagine, I knew him when he was only a bank president." Viktor Frankl actually *found* the humor in that unspeakably tragic situation, and he credits this atti-tude with helping him save his life.

In a similar vein, Vietnam POW Captain Gerald Coffee recounts in his book *Beyond Survival*, how he was at the end of his rope until he noticed a small hole while scrubbing a rat-infested shower stall. Beside the hole read the inscription "Smile – You're On Candid Camera!" And smile he did. That silly little humor zap caused him to laugh uncontrollably and gave him just enough of a changed perspective to give him hope for survival. Coffee also credits humor as a powerful tool for preserving sanity in an insane situation.

So be wary of dismissing humor as trivial. If humor was merely a minor distraction, then it *would* be trivial. But if humor has the power to save lives, change attitudes and foster a broader vision of our world, then surely it can help us create more vibrant, caring and passionate workplaces. (And I still stand by my statement that humor probably makes the coffee taste a whole lot better.)

> *Humor is not only distinctively human, but important to human life in a way that nothing else is.*
> — John Morreall, Professor of Philosophy

— 2 —

Why Humor is Such a Powerful Stress Buster

Men are disturbed not by things, but by the view which they take of them.
— Epictetus, Greek philosopher

I don't want to stress you out, but we all know that stress in the workplace is bad news (the harmful variety, not the catalyst breed we need to fight off grizzlies or win an Olympic gold medal). As most people know, stress is not the problem; it's how we *react* or how our mind *interprets* the *stressors* in our lives that causes problems. In other words, it's not the traffic jam on the way to work that stresses us out, it's our *thoughts* about the traffic jam that cause stress. That's why people with optimistic attitudes and a well-developed sense of humor don't necessarily have less stress in their lives—in fact, they may even have more stressors to deal with—it's that they've chosen to *interpret* the stressors they face in a way that keeps them balanced, sane and happy.

Stress-related absenteeism and illnesses cost the Canadian

economy approximately $12 billion each year and the American economy close to $200 billion. Stress is a morale destroyer, creativity squasher and, ultimately, a people killer. Medical studies report that stress is as dangerous to a person's health as a lack of physical exercise. Prolonged exposure to stress can cause up to 1,500 chemical changes in the body. Stress increases the heart's demand for oxygen, increases body fat, cholesterol and blood pressure, lowers the immune system, kills brain cells and increases the risk of heart disease and cancer. Highly stressed workers have seven times the rate of high blood pressure and heart disease. Stress also increases the incidence of other injuries such as back problems and carpal tunnel syndrome. And if all that isn't bad enough, stress can impede our memory, cloud our thinking, increase the incidents of workplace conflict (1998 U.S. Justice Department figures report 2 million violent workplace episodes per year), play havoc with our hormones and short wire our nervous systems. And where is all our stress coming from? In a recent survey, Canadian and American workers reported that the number one stressor in their lives is the workplace. I'm getting stressed out just thinking about all this.

If you feel you never suffer from the effects of stress, then I am fairly certain a few scientists would like to study you. There is simply no escaping it. We can run, we can hide, but it will find us, and in more shapes and sizes than ever before. Do you remember how, in the good old days, there was just, well, stress? Not anymore. Now there is information fatigue syndrome, techno-stress, cyber-stress, post-stress disorder and delayed stress syndrome. There's road rage, air rage, subway rage, office rage, web rage and even desk rage (whatever happened to just good old-fashioned rage?).

There *are* ways to manage stress. Some of them are illegal (drugs, tossing the photocopier out a 10-story window), while others are highly unethical (putting your boss's tie through the paper shredder). Fortunately, there are also many sane and practical solutions. You can change jobs, set more realistic goals, manage your time better, alter your diet, get more physical exercise, sleep more or practice meditating. Alas, there is no magic pill (no, I do not consider Prozac to be a "magic pill") or simple, short-term solutions to managing stress. The good news, however, is, that many psychologists believe humor is the complete opposite of stress, so you should consider humor a powerful tool to keep handy in your stress-busting repertoire.

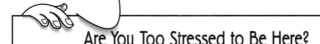

Are You Too Stressed to Be Here?

Here are a few symptoms that could be early warning signs, akin to the canary in the coal mine, that you could be a little overtaxed at work. If you answer yes to three or more of the following, please watch two comedies and call me in the morning.

1. You "cc" the Pope on all your e-mail correspondence.
2. It takes four hours for your hair to unwind at the end of every workday.
3. You wake up screaming only to realize you hadn't fallen asleep yet.
4. You giggle uncontrollably every time you hear the word "buttocks" or "squeegee."
5. You ask the deli to fax you over a bagel.
6. You are beginning to think of Hell as a viable career alternative.

Death By Overwork

The Japanese term karoshi loosely translates into "death by overwork." During the workaholic 1980s, over 10,000 deaths a year were attributed to karoshi in Japan. This, one can only pray, is a bottom line that no organization is striving for.

The Merit of Stress

Here's an ominous sign that stress is infiltrating our lives at an earlier age—the Girl Scouts of America recently unveiled a new merit badge for effective stress management. Now if they could just couple that with a badge for practicing positive humor.

THE COST OF WORKPLACE STRESS
IS STRESSING ME OUT!

There is a myriad of reports, studies and surveys that suggest our level of workplace stress is exacting a costly toll. Here are just a few of their findings:

☂ More people die of heart attacks on Mondays than any other day because of the stress involved in going back to work.

☂ According to *Psychology Today* magazine, 40% of employee turnover is related to stress, and on an average workday, one million American workers are off the job due to stress-related problems.

☂ One out of every three Canadians between the ages of 25 and 44 classified themselves as workaholics in a 1998 Statistics Canada survey.

☂ According to a report by the U.S. Department of Health and Human Service, 18,000 assaults occur weekly in U.S. workplaces.

☂ 24% of people surveyed by the Yale School of Management reported being chronically angry at work.

☂ According to *Alberta Venture* magazine, in 1997, Canadians cited stress and mental anxiety more than physical illness or injury as a reason for workplace absenteeism.

These numbers speak volumes. Of course, you don't need statistics and surveys to know there is a stress epidemic going on. Just look at your co-worker. Right now. The one carrying his computer over to the sixth-story window. Surely, you don't want to end up like him?

 ## Why Laughter Truly is the Best Medicine

Warning: Humor may be hazardous to your illness.
— Ellie Katz

For years, doctors have known that negative emotions, such as anger and worry, affect our physical well-being, yet only recently have they asked the alternative question: What might *positive* emotions do for our well-being? Dr. Norman Cousins was a pioneer in the study of the relationship between our emotions and health, or psychoneuroimmunology (try throwing that little nugget into your next business conversation). His 1979 book *Anatomy of an Illness* outlined his recovery from a "terminal" illness through the use of humor. Dr. Cousins locked himself in a hotel room, where he watched funny videos and prescribed himself a heavy dose of humor therapy, after noticing that a good 20-minute belly laugh gave him two hours of painless rest in the hospital. As Cousins astutely observed, "Laughter is inner jogging."

Cousins was a noted jokester during his stay in the hospital. On one occasion he poured his morning apple juice into his urine sample bottle, then, after remarking to the nurse that his sample was looking a little cloudy, suggested he "run it through" again and poured the "urine" down his throat in front of the dismayed nurse.

Since Cousins' pioneering efforts, other doctors and medical researchers have begun exploring the humor and health connection. Many health researchers now believe that people with a positive, optimistic and humorous attitude get sick less often, and when they do get ill are likely to recover more quickly. We now know that when we experience a good hearty laugh, we:

- relax and reduce tension in our abdomen, shoulder, throat and facial muscles

- massage our internal organs, which aids digestion

- take in six times the normal level of oxygen

- double our heart rate

- lower our blood pressure *(after the laughter subsides)*

- stimulate our nervous system

- improve our circulation

- burn as many calories as during a brisk walk

- reduce our amount of stress-inducing serum cortical

- perhaps trigger an increase in the amount of pain-killing opioids such as endorphins and enkephalins (although this assertion is widely claimed in the popular media, no definitive proof has been found)

- lower our cholesterol
- possibly increase activity in cells that attack tumor cells and viruses
- possibly reduce some headaches, especially tension headaches
- activate T lymphocytes, which in turn boost the immune system
- increase the amount of salivary immunoglobin A, an antibody that helps fight against infections in the upper respiratory track
- possibly mitigate the effects of diseases such as hypertension, heart disease and diabetes
- create a two-step process of stimulation and relaxation by the release of adrenaline and noradrenaline, which reduces inflammation and enhances blood flow
- may reduce or suppress some types of allergies
- improve our lung capacity
- increase production of catecholamines which leads to improved levels of alertness and memory
- carry away toxins (found in cells under stress) in our tears (of laughter *or* sorrow)

Doctors have also discovered that some of the positive effects on our body can last up to 24 hours after a good laugh. Dr. William F. Fry found that just 20 seconds of laughing provides the same cardiovascular workout as 3 minutes on a rowing machine (now I just go to the gym, open up a big bag of potato chips and laugh at the people working out). Dr. Fry actually recommends laughing 100 times a day (6 times per waking hour) – the equivalent caloric workout to 10 minutes of jogging or rowing—as a reasonable prescription for a healthy lifestyle.

News flash: Research suggests a good laugh may be as beneficial as working out on a rowing machine.

Another study found that humor works faster on the body than either Valium or vodka. And yet more research (where subjects held their hands in ice cold water while listening to jokes) shows that humor increases our tolerance for pain (I think that's why James Bond throws out glib one-liners whenever he's being smacked around).

And the wonderful thing about humor is you don't need government or FDA approval to use it! You don't need a permission slip from your doctor, you don't have to stay overnight in the hospital, you don't need an organ transplant, you don't need to see your pharmacist and you sure as heck don't have to walk around in one of those rearview hospital gowns. And as humorist Dale Irwin says, "Laughter is free, legal, has no cholesterol, no preservatives, no artificial ingredients and is absolutely safe!" Furthermore, humor is not bad for the ozone layer, it's not tested on chimps or dogs (at least not to my knowledge), you don't have to sit in a special section in the restaurant, you don't have to sneak it through customs and you don't have to stuff it into the overhead compartment when you fly. You don't need a permit, you don't need to hide it from your parents (or your children) and you don't have to drive across town to use it. Our sense of humor is portable, fully mobile and with us 24 hours a day, 7 days a week, 365 days a year, `til death do us part.

And speaking of `til death do us part, research into longevity suggests that one of the key ingredients to a longer life is the retention of child-like properties into old age, like curiosity, imagination and, of course, a sense of humor. In fact, some researchers suggest that for every 15 seconds we laugh, two days are added to our lifespan. RealAge.com, a web site that features a lifestyle quiz designed to determine our "actual" age as opposed to our chronological age, suggests that laughing a lot can help knock *eight* years off our chronological lives.

Is it any wonder then, that more than a dozen major hospitals in North America have humor programs for patients and their relatives? These range from mobile humor carts (including the Laughmobile, Jokes on Spokes, and Humor a la Cart) that roam the corridors, to hospital clown programs for children (such as The Big Apple Circus Clown Care Unit), to humor rooms where patients and visitors can unwind. There are even humor resources for doctors and nurses, including the *Journal of Nursing Jocularity*, the *Laughter Prescription Newsletter*, the American Association for Therapeutic Humor and the NFL (Nurses for Laughter).

The upshot of all this information is this: introducing more laughter into the workplace *isn't* going to kill us. On the contrary—it's a prescription that just might save our lives.

Laughter is the most inexpensive and most effective wonder drug.

— Bertrand Russell

Always Read the Warning Label

One of the few examples of laughter not being the best medicine occurred when a gentleman who had cardiovascular problems laughed so hard during a **Seinfeld** episode that he fainted three times! (Which reminds me – always read the warning label before reading or listening to any jokes.)

Happy Hearts

According to a recent study by a team of Maryland medical researchers, people with heart disease are 40% less likely to laugh in humorous situations than people with healthy hearts. They found that people with heart disease were much less likely to recognize humor or to laugh, even in positive situations. What still needs a definitive answer, however, is whether humor can help prevent heart disease or whether people with heart disease tend to lose their sense of humor because of the stress of the situation they face.

The Mental Health Benefits of Humor

The greatest discovery of my generation is that human beings can alter their lives by altering the attitude of the mind.

— William James

One of the first signs of a mental health problem such as paranoia or schizophrenia, is the *absence* of humor in a person's life. Failing to find humor in a stressful situation can indicate an overly rigid attitude. By contrast, a healthy dose of silliness in the face of a stressful event is a sign of *good* mental health. (Just consider this simple thought: when was the last time you needed professional help because you were laughing *too* much?)

It shouldn't come as a surprise, then, that in addition to its numerous physical benefits, humor helps us cope mentally with stress. Here are five reasons why humor is such a potent weapon in the battle against stress.

① Humor is the Best Brain Floss Around

When stressed, 70% of our non-dominant brain shuts down, diminishing our senses and our ability to recall or retain information. In short, our brains become fogged up. Often we can make a bad situation worse if we don't take the time to de-fog our brain or reboot its software so that we can tackle what's challenging us with a clear and focused mind. Humor is one of the easiest and most effective ways to clean out those stress-inducing thoughts and redirect our mental energies towards finding solutions.

Humor is the perfect brain floss.

As Milton Berle once said, "Laughter is an instant vacation." Humor, at least for a brief moment, mentally transports us away from the chaos and blows away the mental cobwebs. In short, humor is one of the best forms of mental floss known to humankind.

Worry is the interest we pay on a debt that we may never owe.

— Bill Wolff

② Humor Changes Our Perspective

When we are stressed, we tend to exaggerate. Molehills become mountains, and minor setbacks become international incidents. Why? Because when we're stressed, our mental perspective focuses solely on the problem, magnifying it until it fills our entire mental frame like an enlarged photograph. Soon we imagine that the problem is so bad we will lose our jobs, and then, naturally, we'll have to sell the house, the children and even our feet. When we're thinking this way, it's difficult to find anything to laugh about.

Yet, when we recall some of the funniest moments in our lives, it often brings up events that, at the time, were not remotely funny. We can usually laugh about a crisis or a stressful situation under one of the following conditions:

🌱 *When the crisis is happening to someone else.* As Will Rogers said, "Everything is funny as long as it is happening to someone else." We often laugh at the humorous misfortune of others for the simple reason we are not personally affected by it, and, therefore, have some emotional distance from it.

🌱 *When we have gained distance through time.* Dr. Steve Allen, Jr. reminds us that "Tragedy + Time = Comedy." For minor stressful episodes, a few hours may be all we need before we can laugh, but for larger catastrophes, it may take us months or even years to find some humor in a situation.

🌱 *When we have gained physical distance from the crisis.* Flying to Mexico for a holiday can provide us with enough distance, literally, from a problem to make it easier to find the humor in a stressful situation.

In other words, we can find humor in a stressful event by changing our perspective. We can laugh when enough emotional, temporal or physical space allows us to look at a crisis with a more realistic and broader view. Looking back on a disastrous job interview five years ago, you can laugh about the experience because it now seems so minor in the larger scheme of things. And when you replay the episode of spilling coffee onto the interviewer's lap, you feel like you're watching the events unfold through the eyes of a third party, as though the whole thing happened to someone else.

So humor can help us manage a stressful event while it's happening to us by giving us some much-needed change in perspective. It distances us from stress by removing our tunnel-vision glasses and replacing our perspective with a more peripheral, flexible and realistic view. That's why psychologists consider the ability of patients to laugh at their own problems to be an excellent sign of healing. Patients who can laugh have distanced themselves enough to view their problems from a removed perspective. Humor shatters the magnifying lens focused on an event and reminds us of a few simple facts.

🍄 To err is human and to err is humor. We're all human and people sometimes mess up.

🍄 We're not perfect and neither is life.

🍄 If a meteor the size of Texas was scheduled to collide with our lovely planet next Tuesday, chances are we wouldn't be too worried about our seemingly insurmountable problem.

🍄 Compared to most of the headlines we'll read in tomorrow's paper, this, in all likelihood, isn't a big a deal.

🍄 Although laughing won't solve the problem, neither will being serious, angry or depressed. So you may as well laugh.

And finally, tapping into our humor resources reminds us of a basic truth. We *know* we'll laugh about this bad situation someday, so why miss out? Start laughing now!

The crisis of today is the joke of tomorrow.
— H.G. Wells

③ Humor Gives Us Control Over Our Emotions

When stressed, we are faced with two options—option one: we can lose our cool, blow our tops and set our briefcase on fire; option two: we can find a sane, constructive way of reacting to the stress at hand. Enlisting humor in the fight against stress helps us deal with our *reactions* to stress, since there's often little we can do to completely eliminate the stressors in our work lives. Humor reminds us that although we can't control many of the events that happen to us, we can *always* control our emotions and how we *react* to those events.

Incidentally, most psychologists now denounce the notion that venting our anger is a healthy response, pointing out that it is more likely to lead to heart problems and other stress-related ailments. Venting in a work environment can also be a career-limiting move, especially if the target of your venting is another person (as opposed to the office plant).

In those situations where you feel like exploding, your sense of humor becomes an emergency safety valve, allowing you to release pent-up emotions in a harmless manner. Think of it as an emergency ripcord on a parachute. When you feel your emotions free falling madly out of control, your humor resource will give you a softer landing as you fall gently back to earth. Like shock absorbers on a car, humor won't make the bumps in the road of life go away, but it will make the ride a lot smoother.

Humor also helps combat another major cause of stress—feeling a lack of control over a situation. This lack of control is why workers in lower-ranking jobs with high demands, but little real control or power over their work environment (administrative assistants, clerks and waiters, for example) often feel more stressed than people in higher positions of responsibility. Using humor to control our emotions is a way of exerting power over a situation, and at least regaining control over our own emotions.

> *I refuse to be intimidated by reality anymore.*
> *Reality is just a collective hunch.*
> — Lily Tomlin

④ Humor Restores the Oxygen in a Tense Situation

We've all been in a tense workplace situation, perhaps a boardroom meeting, where someone said something so utterly unbelievable that the entire room stopped talking and the tension became so thick you could pick it up with chopsticks. And then someone said something funny. Or someone's stomach unexpectedly rumbled like an ancient volcano coming out of a deep slumber. And the entire room erupted in laughter and people began breathing again. Suddenly there was oxygen back in the room. This reaction makes sense of our sense of humor from an evolutionary perspective, since laughter may have evolved as a vocal signal for groups to relax once a potentially dangerous situation was determined to be safe. Simply put:

"Ha + Ha + Ha + Ha = Aaaaaaaaaaah."

Humor is a potent combination of icebreaker, conversation starter (or re-starter), rapport builder, unifier, emotional release and perspective changer all rolled into one convenient package. It explains why some mediators use clown noses during conflict resolution sessions. When tensions rise, the mediators have opposing parties don red clown noses and take time out to laugh until riled emotions have settled down. The Troy, New York, police department has even shown up at some domestic conflicts with an officer dressed up as Bugs Bunny to break the tension. And when emotions rose at a meeting attended by Soviet and American officials during the Cuban Missile Crisis, a Soviet delegate suggested that everyone around the table tell a joke or a funny story to clear the impasse. He started with the joke: "What is the difference between capitalism and communism? In capitalism, man exploits man, but in communism, it is the other way around." This humor strategy worked. The talks resumed and the issue was resolved. (So if humor can maintain world peace, just think what it can do for you next Monday morning!)

Against the assault of laughter, nothing can stand.
— Mark Twain

⑤ Humor Elevates Us Above a Crisis

As Viktor Frankl, holocaust survivor and author of *Man's Search for Meaning*, said, "Humor, more than anything else in the human make-up, has an ability to rise above any situation." Humor is an emotional booster and an attitude adjuster that helps us gather our resources to carry on in times when we can't imagine taking one more step. Humor is, quite simply, the fuel that can ignite the inner spirit (am I getting poetic or what?).

Victims of natural disasters will sometimes use humor in this fashion, like the person who, after the 1989 San Francisco earthquake, hammered a sign into the front lawn of his totally demolished home, which read "House For Sale. Some Assembly Required." This is a classic way of rising above a catastrophe. This person, whether he knew it or not, was thumbing his nose at Mother Nature and telling the quake, "You got my house, but you can't get me!" And that, ultimately, is what humor has the power to do for us all.

So now that we know humor is such an effective way to keep our sanity, the next question is *how* can we access our sense of humor during stressful times in our work lives? The answers are coming up in chapter 3 (I couldn't give it all away now, what fun would that be?).

> *Laughter sets the spirit free to move through even the most tragic circumstances. It helps us shake our heads clear, get our feet back under us, and restore a sense of balance and perspective.*
> — Captain Gerald Coffee, POW survivor

Comedy and Tragedy are Next Door Neighbors

In Buddhism, pain and pleasure are two sides of the same coin. Tragedy and comedy are the dual masks symbolizing theater. Both remind us that we just need to flip bad situations around to find some humor in them. Which makes sense, since most comedians and comic writers believe tragedy is a prime hunting ground for humor.

— *3* —

Putting Humor to Work Against Stress

A sense of humor can help you overlook the unat-tractive, tolerate the unpleasant, cope with the unexpected, and smile through the unbearable.
— Moshe Waldoks, co-editor of *The Big Book of Jewish Humor*

Since humor helps us physically and mentally combat stress, how can we muster our humor resources effectively in the face of workplace stress and conflict? Being the simple (and helpful) guy that I am, I've developed a simple formula, known simply as: "The Three Humor R's of Stress Management – Reframe, Reward and Relax."

REFRAME

When a nasty situation rears its ugly head, take a page from stand-up comedians, comedy writers and humorists by mentally reframing the problem or crisis in order to find the humor in it. There are a number of ways to reframe a situation.

1. Wildly Exaggerate. Exaggeration is usually the source of anxiety in a crisis ("I'm going to lose my job!") and why people lose their perspective. Fortunately, as any comedian knows, exaggeration is also a source of much humor. By exaggerating some characteristic about a problem or imagining a worst-case scenario, you can find some humor and regain your perspective by realizing it's probably not as bad as you think.

You can also use exaggeration when faced with a conflict with another person by changing sides in an argument and then wildly exaggerating the other person's point of view. It usually doesn't take long before both sides are finding something to laugh about.

Some therapists use this exaggeration technique to help patients work through serious problems. Viktor Frankl called it "paradoxical therapy," a technique he used with certain patients to get them to laugh at their problems as a way to begin the healing process. Frankl would actually agree that these patients' problems were bad; in fact, he would tell them their problems were *even worse* than they thought. Then, by exaggerating wildly over and over, he would soon reach the point of absurdity that would cause the patient to laugh and gain some perspective on the problem.

2. Step Into Someone Else's Shoes. Reframe the situation by imagining how your favorite comedian, sitcom star or some outlandish fictional character would view the problem. How would Jim Carrey, an alien, Daffy Duck, Xena - Warrior Princess, Charlie Chaplin, James Bond, a five-year-old or Dilbert handle this problem? How would a sitcom writer describe the scene unfolding before you? According to one study, we can reduce our negative responses to things by actually writing out our own sitcom of the events. (I tried this reframing technique once when pulled over for speeding. I put myself in the perspective of Bill Murray, borrowing a line from his movie *Groundhog Day*. When the officer approached my car, I rolled down the window and said, "I'll have a cheeseburger, fries and a banana milkshake." I still got the ticket but I think we both felt better about a stressful situation.)

3. It Can Always Be Worse. Try reframing by imagining, in a humorous way, how things could be worse. Ask yourself, would I be worried about this if a comet was headed for earth? Sometimes you can find the humor simply by completing the following sentence. "It could always be worse, I could be . . ." Or, "Well, the bad news is . . . but the good news is . . ."

This is another standard formula used by comedians to help find something amusing in the worst possible situations. You could also amass a list of wacky-but-true newspaper headlines, strange jobs that make yours seem like a walk in the park or historical blunders as reminders of how things can *always* be worse.

Psychology Today reported on a study that found people who always focused on "how it could have been worse" managed their stress better and remained more positive than those who focused on "how things could have been better." Other studies suggest that people who use a "things could be worse . . ." coping strategy tend to be healthier than those who chronically blame themselves when a stressful event happens.

It <u>Really</u> Can Be Worse!

When you're having one of those days, find solace in the fact that you don't have any of the following real-life jobs (and if you do have one of these jobs, please accept my apologies—I'm confident you've found a way to have fun):

- Poop sniffer – The University of Alberta hired people to sniff pig poop to help researchers determine how far away a barn or pig sty should be located from human dwellings.

- Bull semen collector – yes, it's an actual job. Moooooooooo.

- Bungee cord tester–presumably someone has to be the first to make sure it's working okay.

- Chess tournament play-by-play announcer.

- Sneaker sniffer – researchers hired sniffers to test special odor-sucking socks.

4. Re-label stressors. Invent fun nicknames or code phrases to describe some of the annoying stressors that frequently pop up in your workplace. The employees of a company I worked with devised a reframing technique for dealing with annoying customers. In order to keep their attitudes upbeat, they developed a code for different types of problem clients. For example, "16" might refer to an overly obnoxious individual, while "11" was someone with severe garlic breath. As the employees would pass each other, they would quietly say, "I'm helping a '16' right now, can I talk to you later about this?" This was their simple way of reframing a stressor in a more humorous light.

These are just a few ideas. When we mentally reframe something, we are tapping into the power of our imagination, so the possibilities are truly limitless.

> *A sense of humor is a sense of proportion.*
> — Kahil Gibran

The Humor Flip-Flop

Humor can help us execute a quick "flip-flop" reframe during a stressful situation. Winston Churchill was a master of this. Lady Astor, when she became frustrated with Churchill during a heated conversation, told him, "Sir Winston, if I was your wife I would put arsenic in your coffee." Churchill used a humor flip-flop by responding, "Madam, if I was your husband, I'd drink it." Likewise, a speaker who, after tripping over an extension cord, immediately pops back onto her feet and says, "Wow, I got a perfect 10 from the Romanian judge!" is using a humor flip-flop to turn around a potentially embarrassing situation.

It's even possible to create a list of generic humor flip-flop phrases to cover a whole range of potentially stressful situations. Here's a sample of some all purpose lines. For the best effect, though, create your own flip-flop recovery line and only use it in the most positive, warmest tone (non-sarcastic) possible!

"I'd rather be . . . "	"Did I fill out the wrong form today?"
"Beam me up – NOW, Scotty."	"Wasn't this a *Twilight Zone* episode?"
"It takes a special human being to do what I just did."	"This is great, I was feeling a little under-stressed today."
"Can I have a standing ovation please?"	"Where's my stunt double?"
"Can we re-shoot this whole scene from the start?"	"This just isn't my millennium."
"Are we on *Candid Camera*?"	"Hey Regis, can I use a lifeline?"
"I knew I should have turned left at that last corner."	"Is it tomorrow yet?"
"I really didn't order this."	"I'm quite certain the weatherman said nothing about this."
"Was today really necessary?"	"If you're going to mess up, I always said, go big or go home!"
"Can I go for what's behind door number 1 instead?"	

There cannot be a crisis next week, my schedule is full.
— Henry Kissinger

Words to Laugh By

As seen on many a helpful sign: "Life is a test. Life is only a test. If this had been your actual life, you would have been given better instructions."

Does Reframing Really Help?

According to author Mihaly Csikszentmihalyi, there are three factors contributing to how we cope with stress: external support, such as friends and family; psychological resources, which include our intelligence and personality traits; the coping strategies we use when confronted with stress. Of the three, Csikszentmihalyi suggests the third, how we cope with stress, is the most important. This is the factor most under our control, and many people have overcome major life tragedies and obstacles simply by reframing how they viewed the stressor. By looking at them as potential challenges, or using other "transformational coping" techniques, some people have even viewed life-altering events, such as becoming blind or paralyzed, as positive events that enriched their lives.

Humor is emotional chaos remembered in tranquility.
— James Thurber

Reframing the Big "C"

The late comedy-writer Marjorie Gross wrote about her experience fighting cancer. To help her humorously reframe her battle, she compiled a list of the advantages of having cancer, which included:

You automatically get called courageous.

People immediately return your calls.

You never get called rude again.

No one ever asks you to help them move.

Laughter rises out of tragedy when you need it the most and rewards you for your courage.
— Erma Bombeck

REWARD

Many people mistakenly believe that the only time they deserve a reward is when something good has happened. (Now don't get me wrong, it's important to reward yourself and each other for successes in the workplace. In fact, a substantial portion of chapter 7 is devoted to that very topic.) But when do you really *need* a little injection of fun, humor and laughter in your life? When is humor going to be the most beneficial and welcome? It's when your computer crashes or your boss dumps an assignment on you on a Friday afternoon that you really need an injection of fun. So find ways to reward yourself the next time you are confronted with a workplace stressor – especially by things truly beyond your control.

One believer is the store manager, who, unhappy with the poor service given to some difficult customers, offers a free dinner once a week to whoever best serves the "customer from Hell."

Another company set up a bin of chocolate treats, accessible *only* when a passing train (a major source of stress in this small office) roars by. Other companies have even started programs that reward employees for having all-round bad days. For example, Windsor Canadian Whiskey has sponsored "Worst Workday" contests. The winner one year was Harry Glass from Pasadena, Texas. While delivering an outdoor talk on safety and the need to wear protective gear at all times, a bird deposited a glob of do-do right on the top of Harry's noggin. (He was holding his hard hat in his hands just as he was stressing the need to wear them at all times.)

So remember what those ever-so-happy motivational speakers are always preaching: "Stressed spelled backwards is desserts," and the next time your computer crashes or a bird pays your head an unexpected visit, grab yourself an extra serving of double chocolate cheesecake – you deserve it. (Just don't turn it into a habit – otherwise you'll have a whole host of other stressors to worry about!)

Sometimes All You Can Do is Laugh

Laughter and tears are both responses to frustration and exhaustion . . . I myself prefer laughter since there is less cleaning up to do afterward.
— Kurt Vonnegut

When life delivers you a bouquet of rotten skunks or you've tried your best and your best just didn't seem to come anywhere close to qualifying for the finals, then sometimes, all you really can do is laugh. And then remind yourself you deserve a reward just for getting out of bed that morning.

Some organizations have formalized this concept of laughing at our blunders through fun, lighthearted awards. The International Association of Professional Bureaucrats doles out the "Order of the Featherless Bird" award for bureaucratic bungling, while the Ontario Newspaper Association has a blooper award as part of its annual awards.

So here are a few deep, and not-so-deep, thoughts about the art of messing up, reminding us that sometimes, when things run amuck, all we can do is laugh.

The average millionaire has been bankrupt three times.

"No one is ever listening . . .until you make a mistake."
Anon.

"It takes a wise man to learn from his own mistakes, but an absolute idiot not to learn from the mistakes of others."
TV's Dr. Frasier Crane

Reggie Jackson, one of the greatest home run hitters in baseball, also struck out more than anyone in history – a total of 2,597 times.

"If you want to succeed, double your failure rate."
Tom Watson, IBM chairman

"Failure is not a crime. Failure to learn from failure is."
Walter Wriston, Citicorp chairman

"Success occurs in private, failure in full view."
Anon.

"All of my discoveries were made by mistake. You discover what is by getting rid of what isn't."
Buckminster Fuller

"You may be disappointed if you fail, but you are doomed if you don't try."
Beverly Sills

"Experience is something you don't get until after you need it."
Anon.

"If at first you do succeed, you'll get a false sense of security."
Thoreau

"I failed my way to success."
Thomas Edison

"If you learn to laugh at yourself, you'll never run out of things to laugh at."
Leo Buscaglia

A good laugh and a long sleep are the best cures.
— Irish proverb

RELAX

The final "R" is the granddaddy of the three humor R's of stress management – *RELAX!* You need to find ways to access your sense of humor when the going gets tough. And, by no means, is this an easy thing to do. After all, it may be child's play to laugh when things are great, but it's a lot more difficult when we have to get through those layers of anger, frustration and anxiety that blanket us during a stressful ordeal. Difficult, but by no means impossible.

To be humorously prepared for your next stressful ordeal, ask yourself, "What, *especially* in the face of stress, is going to make me laugh?" Considering that our sense of humor is as unique as our fingerprints, this is a question that only you can answer. In fact, try this right now. Grab a piece of paper and write down five things that might make you laugh in a stressful situation. Remember, there are lots of humor aids ("HA's") to help you access your humor—toys, funny photographs, silly props, cartoon books, comedy tapes, funny hats—the list is endless. And since your humor resource has the power to make you feel better, like an injection of medicine, you can even create your own "humor first aid kit," filling it with the items you've identified as your humor aids. Put your humor first aid kit in your desk drawer, briefcase or car for the commute home. And the next time you begin to feel a little stressed, reach for the kit and give yourself an instant shot of humor. (It may sound silly, but then humor often is, isn't it?)

A clown is like aspirin only he works twice as fast.
— Groucho Marx

A Laughing Epidemic?

India is the birthplace of a unique, some might even say amusing, phenomenon. Taking advantage of laughter's therapeutic values and its contagious properties, Laughter Clubs have sprung up throughout urban centers in India. There are at least 400 clubs in India, more than 50 in Bombay alone, with a total membership of 25,000 (and growing) laugh-aholics.

The idea originated with Dr. Madan Kataria, a Bombay physician. From his initial laugh club involving a few friends, people of all walks of life, including doctors, business managers, shopkeepers and clerks, now gather in parks or parking lots throughout India—and laugh. Most clubs meet regularly each morning for 20 minutes, where as many as 50 to 100 people begin their day on the right attitudinal footing with a good chuckle-fest.

When the clubs began, participants told jokes to initiate the laughter. However, the jokes soon became stale and people found some of them offensive, so they did away with the joke portion and moved straight to the laughter (heck, why waste all that time?). Dr. Kataria firmly believes that, just as a sense of humor leads to more laughter, the corollary is also true: laughter helps us develop our sense of humor.

Although there are some variations, the standard routine at a laughter club begins with some deep-breathing exercises, then a group chant in unison, "Ho-Ho-Ha-Ha-Ho-Ho-Ha-Ha . . .," which slowly increases in speed. Next, members run through a medley of seven different types of laughs (including the hearty laugh, dancing laugh, swinging laugh and cocktail laugh). The forced laughter soon gives way to an epidemic of spontaneous giggles, chuckles and guffaws, and participants leave the session feeling refreshed, relaxed, revitalized and re-energized. Many members ➤

claim that the laughter clubs have changed their entire outlook on life. In fact, 72% of Laughter Club members report improved interpersonal relations with co-workers, 85% say it has improved their self-confidence and 66% suggest it has improved their ability to concentrate.

The Laughter Club phenomenon has started to infect workplaces as well. Workers begin each day at the Electrical Products of India company with a hearty laugh-fest. Company managers report a significant improvement in interpersonal relationships, a reduced incidence of workplace colds and headaches and increased productivity.

These clubs are starting to form in cities all over the world, including North America where there is accredited training in laughter club leadership through the World Laughter Tour Incorporated. You can visit the homepage of the Laughter Club International at www.worldlaughtertour.com

> *If we couldn't laugh we would all go insane.*
> — Jimmy Buffet

Here are some more suggestions for ways to access your sense of humor and relax.

1. Make a silly face. Better yet, pull out a mirror so you can see yourself making a silly face. No, you're right, it's not very professional, but it is a quick and painless way to tap into the five-year-old inside you and remind yourself not to take life too seriously.

2. Start smiling. Researchers believe that even fake smiling (although *not* the teeth-gritted "I'm going to kill you" kind of smiling) can bring about the same beneficial physical changes that occur when we really smile.

3. Start laughing. Literally, just start to laugh. Sure, this sounds like you're putting the humor cart before the horse. (You probably thought that first you needed something to laugh at, then the laughter would follow.

How silly of you). But guess what? If you just start laughing (not in the middle of a business presentation, mind you) soon you *will* be laughing at something—yourself! You can do it alone, or better yet with some of your colleagues. Laughter is, after all, thought to be one of the most highly contagious phenomena known to humankind (which is why most TV sitcoms come with fake laugh tracks).

4. Take regularly scheduled humor breaks. The Caribbean slang term "liming" means to just "hang out, chill, or do nothing in a guilt-free way." Liming once a day, with a twist of humor, sounds like the perfect recipe for coping with a stressful day. So find someone to share a joke with, read a funny magazine or listen to a tape of a comedian. People who take short breaks usually end up accomplishing more by the end of a workday because they're less fatigued and less stressed and they make fewer mistakes. Even short breaks give our brains time to digest information and to play catch up. Think of these breaks not as time *off*, but as time *out* from your hectic schedule.

Even taking a short "mental vacation" helps. Visualizing a humorous moment or mentally reliving a hilarious incident can lower your heart rate and reduce your blood pressure.

5. Stockpile your favorite comedian's jokes or cartoon books. Pick your favorite three books and keep them on your office bookshelf or in your desk for easy reference.

6. Make me laugh! Don't feel you have to manage your stress alone. Talking, and better yet, laughing with someone else is an extremely effective de-stressor. It often helps to talk to people totally unrelated to your immediate work environment, so find the nearest five-year-old, grab someone from accounting or phone a buddy and say, "Make me laugh!" You'll be amazed at how imaginative people are and how quickly you *will* start laughing over the simplest things. (When I give people this exercise in workshops, it rarely takes more than five seconds to get uproarious laughter from the partner who has been instructed to *not* laugh at all costs!)

7. Humorize your office environment. It's difficult to access your sense of humor in a somber physical work environment. Studies of prisoners, submarine crews, hospital patients, office workers and even rodents have all led to the same basic conclusion: our physical surroundings have a tremendous impact on our creativity, mood, attitude and productivity. The rodent study is my favorite. One set of rodents was placed in a dull, stark environment, while another group lived in a lively, colorful environment full of toys, mazes, ladders and mental stimuli. The results? The rodents in the stark environs lost brain cells, while the other rodents actually grew brain cells. The stimulated rodents had an average of 40,000 more neurons and 20% more dendritic branching in their brains. (*I'm pretty certain one of them ended up on the game show Jeopardy!*)

So liven up the office. Put up humorous posters, pictures or signs. Keep a wacky company mascot on display. Create a humor bulletin board where employees can post funny photos, wacky stories or top-10 lists. Display a funny quote or humorous question of the day in a highly traveled corridor. Program your computers to play fun music when they are turned on. Create fun walls of employee photos with changeable thought balloons coming out of their heads that folks can switch throughout the week.

8. Switch brains (and no, not with someone else). You can reduce stress by switching to an activity that uses the part of your brain not causing you stress. For example, if the source of your stress is centered in the creative and emotional right hemisphere (you are depressed, anxious, worried or otherwise emotionally distraught), then change to a task that requires more of your left hemisphere to kick in, such as doing some accounting (yippee!), organizing or writing in a journal. Conversely, if the stress is a result of being time pressured or overworked, chances are your left hemisphere is stressed. In this case, do a right-brain activity, like engaging in play or a creative pursuit.

9. Create a humor room. Kodak-Eastman, Hewlett-Packard and many other companies have humor or "lighten up" rooms, which are essentially playrooms for stressed-out executives, as a way to help employees unwind and access their humor. The rooms are stocked with comedy videos, humorous books, toys—anything that helps employees tap into their humor resources.

10. Collect funny props. A visit to a toy store, magic shop or joke store will provide some inspiration for things to keep on hand in your office or boardroom to use for "serious" emergencies. Or scour your home. A photograph of your dog dressed in a tuxedo, a picture of you when you were three or that strange gizmo your brother-in-law found in Bora Bora might be just the ticket for tickling your funny bone.

11. Stockpile funny costume items. It doesn't matter whether it's a clown nose, elf ears, sombrero, shower cap, bonehead headband, beanie cap, fake rotting teeth or a Hawaiian lei—if it makes you laugh, then keep it close at hand. Items like these have inspired many people to access their sense of humor. An office in Los Angeles for example, has a de-stressing ritual at the end of each workday. At quitting time, employees gather in the open office, don cherry-red clown noses and say good night to each other. They continue wearing their noses as they leave the building and drive home, only removing them once safely home. It's their silly way of saying: "We're not taking ourselves too seriously and we sure as heck aren't going to carry any of today's stress home with us." There is also a group of New York stockbrokers that belongs to the Secret Order of the Mickey Mouse Club, complete with Mickey Mouse boxer shorts underneath their suits. And Canadian astronaut Julie Payette even managed to sneak a clown nose into space during her 1999 space shuttle mission.

12. Get moving! It's been determined that the simple act of thrusting our arms above our heads raises our spirits. Children are naturals at this. I work next door to a preschool (which explains a lot, I'm sure). One day while walking through the preschool, I noticed a child spinning madly in one direction, giggling his little heart out. "What the heck are you doing?" I asked. "Spinning," he replied. (I often overlook the obvious.) "Why?" I asked. "Why not?" he responded. The point is, sitting behind a desk all day we forget to engage our bodies in the fight against stress, yet using our bodies is an obvious way to access our sense of humor *and* dampen our stress levels.

One company I worked with had a stress-busting ritual that went like so: when people were frustrated and in need of a little levity, they would spring up out of their desk, run to a bell, ring it madly and turn on some music. The bell ringing was everyone's cue to stop what they were doing, leap onto their desks and start dancing. It didn't matter what style of dance, people did their own wacky thing. Sure it sounds crazy, but it's pretty difficult to feel stressed and depressed in an office full of dancing people.

Of course, putting your body in motion doesn't have to be this involved. I once worked with a fellow who, whenever we met up in the hallway, would enthusiastically yell out, "Bounce with me Mikey!" And we started bouncing. We bounced as people walked by. We bounced in the stairway. We bounced with our briefcases. The point is we bounced. Our bouncing became a ritual and, as silly as it sounds, a simple way to access our humor and literally bounce away some of our stresses.

• • • • • • • • • •

These ideas are merely the tip of the humor iceberg. With a little practice and a little persistence, you *can* combat the effects of stress through humor. The real trick to all this is painfully simple: give yourself *permission* to play, have fun, be a little silly and laugh.(And if that doesn't work, take a couple of humor breaks and call me in the morning.)

You Deserve a Humor Break

Play is essential for life . . . it is not selective, it is mandatory.
— Dr. O. Carl Simonton

If you find it difficult to relax or take a "humor break" for fear that you'll fall behind on the old rat race, or you simply can't afford the time, remind yourself that the opposite is true. The reality is, at those times when you are busiest and most stressed out, you can't afford *not* to take a break.

Workaholics are rarely productive in the long run. Besides sacrificing their personal health and family lives, workaholics who run themselves into the ground don't usually perform as well as people who take regular breaks. A study from the Pittsburgh School of Medicine found workers' chances of a heart attack are 30% higher if they haven't taken a vacation in the last year. To be efficient, healthy and truly productive, people *need* regular breaks.

Too often, however, when the work piles up people turn into the "Clint Eastwoods" of the corporate world, believing the key to success is rolling up their sleeves, spitting on the ground, squinting their eyes and working 27-hour workdays. This attitude is unfortunately viewed by many as a badge of honor, with workers bragging about who's working the hardest. "Yeah," these folks smugly say, "The next six weeks, I'll be at the office 24/7. I won't eat, I won't go to the bathroom and I sure as heck won't be sleeping." And at the end of the six weeks, they stagger across the finish line. And *then*, they say to themselves, it's time for a little break. But when people work too long in this mode, their stress increases, they're prone to more errors, creativity plummets and productivity decreases. Although it may *look* like workaholics are working harder, the reality is that they often accomplish less because they're typically more focused on the work itself, *not* on the results.

Gymboree Corp. takes *their* fun breaks seriously. On Wednesdays, it's company snack time; on Thursdays, it's recess time, when employees are encouraged to go outside and play. During this 20-minute or longer break (announced by a ringing bell), you might find staff playing hop scotch or with Hula Hoops. As reported by Amy Post in the *Washington Post*, these breaks stir creativity, foster a climate of teamwork and instill a sense of tremendous loyalty amongst the employees.

So we need to view a "humor break" as a much-needed time out—a time out where our brains can get recharged and our spirits replenished. Play is just too important to our normal development, health and sanity to leave it to chance.

> *Every now and then go away, even briefly, have a little relaxation, for when you come back to work, your judgment will be surer, to remain constantly at work will cause you to lose your power.*
> — Leonardo da Vinci

— 4 —

The Office Commute – May the Farce Be With You

Even the term "commute" seems to be filled with a sense of foreboding (it sounds like a tropical disease – "I've just come down with a bad case of *commute*"). For many of us, the daily drive into the office sets the tone for the entire day, while the commute home molds our mood for the evening ahead with loved ones. Bad weather, inconsiderate drivers (a polite euphemism for $*&$* drivers), too many drivers, car trouble, pot holes the size of Belgium, bicycle couriers riding at the speed of the space shuttle and too much wasted time are just a few of the potential stressors awaiting the office commuter. But wait, it gets even better—or is that worse?

Today, with the miracle of technology, we've brought the office to the car. Now as you cruise the highway you can simultaneously cruise the information highway. You can chat on the phone, e-mail messages, fax important documents and monitor your progress to work via your car's on-board computer, all the while holding a decaffeinated low-fat double espresso precariously between your thighs (and I can still remember the days of going for a drive to get away from it all). No wonder so many workers complain they are stressed out before they even enter the workplace. And unfortunately, psychologists believe that the first hour, for many workers, the commuting hour, plays a huge role in setting the tone for the entire day.

WHY IS ROAD RAGE ALL THE RAGE?

Road rage has become a household term for the simple reason that it's happening more and more frequently. Drivers find it easy to vent frustrations because of the anonymity afforded by being isolated in a huge tin box. And it's not just men who are losing their cool, either. As women face more stressful work lives, their participation in the road rage craze is approaching the level of men's.

In her research into road rage, as reported in *Psychology Today*, Dr. Nancy Herman found women were getting more aggressive behind the wheel as a result of moving up the corporate ladder. She concluded that, regardless of gender, "oppressive conditions and alienation in the workplace lead people to misdirect their anger when they drive." This is another sober reminder of how workplace stresses carry over into other parts of our lives.

Herman also discovered that 63% of road rage offenders feel it's not their fault, that road rage is an inborn trait and therefore beyond their control. Most psychologists don't buy this argument. We are always in control of how we *interpret* the stressors we face. So if you are a road warrior, consider some of the following emergency roadside humor fixes to remind yourself that when it comes to your own emotions, you truly are in the driver's seat.

ROADSIDE ASSISTANCE WITH A SMILE

Without humor, more people will be shooting each other on the expressway.
— Dan Piraro, Bizarro cartoonist

1. Look for creative ways to lighten up your car's physical environment. Put funny pictures or stress-relieving silly buttons on the dashboard (Ejection Seat Launcher!, Warp Drive!, or Instant Espresso Maker) or hang a "Lighten Up!" reminder

symbol from the rear-view mirror.

2. Create a technology-free zone. A recent newspaper article reported how a poor gentleman in South Korea died after he walked into a tree while talking on his cell phone. Now think about all those folks jabbering away in their cars at high speeds. The *Journal of New England Medicine* has thought about it; in fact, it's concluded there's four times the risk of a car accident when people are talking on their cell phones. Let's face it, driving is challenging enough, so creating a technology-free zone and focusing on the road is an obvious way to lighten your stress load and keep you in a more positive mind-set for the office. If you feel the need to maintain your image, most toy stores carry plastic cell phones for under $10. Or better yet, invest in a toy walkie-talkie, then people will think you are *really, really* important.

3. Listen to comedy tapes or humorous novels on cassettes.

4. Find silly ways to relax when the going *doesn't* get going. Sing your favorite songs or make up your own songs, don a clown nose if the traffic backs up, make goofy faces, or sing along to the news or traffic reports.

5. Watch for humorous bumper stickers, highway signs or billboards and start your own file to share with your co-workers. You could have an ongoing office contest for the best bumper sticker spotted each month. And don't forget to share your own humor with other drivers by posting a humorous sticker on your vehicle (more than 70 web sites are available on the internet where you can order pre-made or customized bumper stickers). With a little imagination, your office could even devise humorous bumper stickers for your work vehicles.

Some of my favorite bumper stickers include:

I'd Give My Right Arm To Be Ambidextrous
Only One Shopping Day Left Until Tomorrow
I Don't Suffer From Insanity—I Enjoy Every Minute of It!
The Problem With Sex In The Movies Is Usually The Popcorn Spills
He Who Laughs Last—Thinks Slowest
NEVER Believe Generalizations
It's Lonely at the Top. What, Like It's a Big Party at the Bottom?
Give Me Ambiguity or Give Me Something Else
In Only Two Days It Will Be the Day After Tomorrow

Ever Stop to Think and Forget to Start Again?
If At First You Don't Succeed . . . Skydiving Is NOT For You
It's 98% of the Politicians That Give the Rest a Bad Name
Forget World Peace. Visualize Using Your Turn Signal.
Hang Up and Drive!
Smiling is the Second Best Thing You Can Do With Your Lips

Commuting Humor Isn't Just for Cars

As reported in The Humor Project's LAUGHING MATTERS magazine, a reader shared how commuters on a bus and train commute started bringing in a cartoon-of-the-day to share with fellow passengers. This is a great reminder that commuting humor knows no boundaries, so whether you travel by car, plane, rickshaw or gondola, find some creative ways to make the journey as fun as possible.

Insulting Fines

A German court banned a 22-year-old man from driving for four and a half months and fined him $1,400 Canadian for shouting "typical female" at a woman driver. He claimed he was provoked after the woman screamed "young whipper-snapper!" If only they'd read this chapter . . .

6. Humorously reframe those annoying drivers by picturing them as the actual insult you are about to hurl at them (e.g., visualize the "bonehead" in front of you—what *would* an *actual real-life* bonehead look like? Or how about that jackass driving the VW? And then there's that pinhead in the Jaguar who just cut you off . . .)

7. Hold a contest and award a prize for the "Best Commute From Hell Story" to reward someone who really needs it or give a prize for the "Funniest Commuting Story." Relate the prizes to commuting, like a humorous audio tape, bumper sticker or mirror ornament.

8. If you car pool, start up some traditions like these.

   🍸 Begin each Monday morning with a joke or funny story. Award a free coffee and donut for the best joke or story.
   🍸 Have a contest to see who can guess what color underwear everyone in the car pool is wearing.

- Hold a trivia contest to see who pays for the morning coffee.
- Play the "license plate" game, where everyone has to make a word out of the license plate letters on the car ahead of you.
- Create a scavenger hunt for things to watch for on the way to the office (this doesn't just work with kids, trust me).
- Play "Whose Head will Fit in the Glove Compartment?" a fun game that is sure to make the hours pass by quickly. (I'm kidding! This is David Letterman's idea—don't try it or I know one of you will get your head stuck and sue me.)
- Have a "theme" pool. If it works for parties or offices, why not car pools? Once a month have everyone dress as the Blues Brothers or wear clown noses. Or make it a carPOOL party and dress in your favorite beach wear. It doesn't matter what you do, as long as it starts a good tradition and breaks everyone out of their routine.

9. If you get pulled over for speeding (I know, highly *unlikely* with you) or stopped in a routine roadside check, use some humor to lighten up the situation. Offer the kind police officer a "Get Out of Jail Free" Monopoly card (stored for just such an occasion in your wallet) or show them a picture of your "pride and joy" (joke stores sell wallet-sized photos of actual bottles of "Pride" wax and "Joy" dishwasher detergent).

10. Share some good humor with other folks along the way. It's amazing how much a small token can make a difference to *your* own mood as well. So if you see a toll booth operator each day or a flag person along a highway construction zone, share a quick joke or offer them one of your morning donuts.

IMPROVISING YOUR ROAD RAGE AWAY

The American Institute for Public Safety (AIPS) uses an innovative technique to teach people to manage their road rage. Through its Improv Traffic Schools, the AIPS uses humor and theater improvisational games to help participants relax, role play scenarios and retain the information presented to them. A two-year study carried out in Florida found that participants in the improv classes had fewer traffic violations and car accidents than students in the traditional classrooms.

In a similar vein, a California court directs road ragers and other traffic violators to visit a driver's ed school (in lieu of a ticket) with a bit of a twist. At a few rather unique schools, stand-up comedian/trainers help wayward drivers role play different scenarios in a fun way, while a "jury" hurls lighthearted insults at them about their bad driving habits. There are several of these humor-based traffic schools throughout the U.S., including the Better Value Comedy Traffic School, the License to Laugh Traffic School and the Court Jesters Defensive Driving School. So if you feel a little refresher training in defensive driving could dampen your commuting stress, why not look for a program that throws in a few chuckles along the journey?

"Now **that's** the way to carpool."

HUMOROUS HELP ON THE WEB

Rather than raging on the paved highway, vent on the information highway in the safety of your own home. Several web sites dedicated to stopping road rage can be found, such as www.stop-road-rage.com. Some of the sites allow you to submit observations of deranged drivers: at www.members.aol.com/doggiesnot/ you'll find "How to Drive Like a Moron" where you can report highway morons. You can also print out a package of "Moron Summons," which allows you to ticket people with a "Driving or Parking Like a Moron" certificate outlining your complaint. Other sites to check out include:

DUDS, Data Base of Unsafe Drivers
www.comnet.ca/~chezken/duds.html

Bloody Idiots
www.geocities.com/Baja/9799/

License to Laugh Traffic School
www.members.aol.com/licens2laf/lic2laf.html
(includes humorous insurance report excuses)

If you submit a bad road experience to a web site, be sure to add a humorous twist to your tale. It will help you distance yourself even further from your anger and give other road ranters a chuckle as well.

A SALUTE TO ALTERNATIVE SOLUTIONS

The official gesture of the road rage age is of course the old "waving-without-using-all-of-our-fingers" signal. In an effort to promote friendlier behavior on the highways, Governor Roy Romer of Colorado suggested a two-finger salute to replace the more traditional one. He hopes that the two-finger "hello/thanks/no-problem/I-noticed-you-were-about-to-smash-into-me" salute will encourage people to open their hearts and be a little more gracious and generous while driving.

Electronic signs that hang from the rear window and flash messages to tailgaters are another possible rage-reducing aid. Design 21 FX Lighting, an Edmonton, Alberta, based company, distributes these signs that, with the flick of a switch on your dashboard, flash "SORRY," "THANKS" or "HELP" (but curiously, there are no signs that flash "Where did you learn to drive?").

One last, frightening solution comes in the guise of emotional computer technology. Futuristic technology folks are talking about computers that will one day interpret our emotions. They claim these computers, with such nifty attachments as the "emotional mouse," will let us know when we need to take it easier on the computer or when our boss is in an irate mood. When attached to our vehicles, this technology could ward off road rage by serving as an early detection system. For example, when the computer decides we have passed our emotional threshold, it will play soothing music, prevent us from honking the horn, or maybe even start throwing out a few one-liners to lighten our stress load. (As much as I like wacky solutions, just driving sanely and learning to laugh more seems a little simpler, and lot more fun.)

A CLOSING THOUGHT

Comedian George Carlin puts the topic of commuter stress in a fresh and oh-so-true perspective by offering these sage words of wisdom: "Have you noticed that when you are driving, everyone driving faster than you is a maniac, while everyone driving slower than you is a moron?"

Happy trails folks. And may the farce be with you.

— 5 —

Laughing in the Face of Change

I could not tread these perilous paths in safety if I did not keep a sense of humor.
— Lord Neilson

Managing change is an umbrella for a whole range of workplace issues. Change is a major source of stress and an issue that touches on motivation, communication and creativity. Once again, our trusted sense of humor can help us through the fog that sometimes engulfs us during times of massive change. Humor deflects some of the stress associated with change, keeps motivation levels high, facilitates open communication and helps organizations be more innovative so that change becomes the norm, not an earth-shattering experience that only rears its head every 10 years or so.

SLAYING THE DRAGONS

If you want to thrive and remain competitive in a world that is changing radically and relentlessly, you need the fluidity and flexibility of humor.
— C.W. Metcalf, humor author

People resist change for a whole host of reasons, ranging from not understanding what exactly is changing to failing to see any reason to do things differently. The overriding reason most people resist change, however, is fear—fear of failure, fear of success, fear of risk, and, especially, fear of the unknown. Doing what we've always done is like wearing an old sweater. It's comfortable. It's cozy. It's familiar. It's safe. Throwing out that old sweater for something we've never tried on before can seem downright frightening.

Humor has always been a powerful weapon in the face of change and unknown boogey men. Woody Allen's favorite comedic subject matter is the greatest unknown of all—death. As Allen quips, "I'm not sure if there is an afterlife, but I'm not taking any chances. I'm bringing an extra pair of underwear along just in case." By joking about death, Allen cuts through our fear of the unknown and makes us see death in a less-frightening light. Another Woody Allen quote reminds us it's possible to find humor in hopeless situations: "More than any time in history, mankind faces a crossroad. One path leads to despair and utter hopelessness, the other to total extinction. I just pray that we have the wisdom to choose correctly."

Applying heavy doses of humor can make major change seem less daunting. Like the old sugar with the cough syrup trick, humor can help employees swallow the distasteful parts of change a whole lot easier. At its best, heaps of humor and fun can make a massive change in the workplace seem like a great adventure that the entire organization is taking together. Here are four guiding lights for effectively managing change à la humor in the workplace.

① Communication is Everything

The more you communicate the fewer unknowns there are. Some managers spend 70 to 90% of their time during massive periods of change doing nothing but explaining and selling the change to employees. The key messages to communicate are why the change is happening, the benefits of the change and the risks associated with *not* changing. Good managers also take the time to communicate the things that *aren't* going to change. Communicating all this information is the perfect opportunity to add heavy doses of humor so staff are motivated to get involved in the change and the change is less stressful. For example, you might consider:

🍄 Writing a humorous newsletter to introduce the change, perhaps spoofing a tabloid magazine.

☂ Creating a list of the "Top 10 Reasons to Change" or the "Top 10 Good Things About Our New _____." Make it fun and include a few wacky red herrings to keep people smiling.

☂ Putting together a video for staff, replete with "staff-in-the-hall" interviews, with some fun examples of how the change will personally affect employees. Show some outlandish and exaggerated reactions to highlight how excited people are (screaming down the hallway like a wild banshee always seems to work well) about the change.

☂ Establishing a fun talk show or "town hall" format meeting with some entertaining segments and plenty of opportunities for staff to ask questions in an upbeat, non-threatening atmosphere.

☂ Helping staff to humorously reframe their stress about the changes by preparing a list highlighting the "Bad News is . . ." versus the "Good News is . . ." This technique presents a more balanced perspective and lightheartedly acknowledges some of the concerns employees may have.

☂ Incorporating humor into any staff training that is required to introduce the change. Training is intimidating for most people, so make it as playful and non-threatening as possible. Create humorous handouts using participants' actual names in case-study examples, incorporate fun videos, use role plays or develop a quiz-style, game-show format to test people's knowledge about the changes taking place.

☂ Developing a fun slogan to promote the change and posting it everywhere and anywhere, including the doors of toilet stalls, coffee mugs, T-shirts and office bulletin boards (or heck, go wild and have the CEO tattoo it on her forehead). Or create movie-style posters announcing some of the changes with captions like "Coming Soon to an Office Near You" or "Soon to Be Released . . ."

☂ Reminding people to eliminate idea-busting phrases (see chapter 6) in a fun way. Display your most common idea busters, circulate them and create a fun penalty for violators.

☂ Allowing staff to give their opinions of the change. During massive periods of change, sometimes staff simply need to know their concerns are being heard, which may mean they need to express themselves or even to vent. And yes, you *can* make venting a fun experience. Stage a "whine and cheese" party to let people voice their concerns in a fun "open mike" setting. One Hewlett-Packard plant hired a jazz band and held a mock funeral to help their employees grieve the closure of a division. If you hold events like this, keep them light, without diminishing the concerns or emotions staff may be genuinely feeling, and follow up with a celebration of the upcoming changes.

② Create a Burning Bridge

Give people a compelling reason to change by creating a sense of urgency. Explain the benefits of changing *and* the consequences of not changing. Encourage staff to embrace the changes by developing some fun rewards for actively participating in the change and fun penalties for not. You could, for example, offer wacky rewards for the first employee or entire department to adopt a new practice or new technology. As a leader, don't forget to be open about any setbacks, failures or bumps along the journey and don't be afraid to poke fun at the top brass. People need to know it's okay to laugh at honest mistakes when doing something new.

③ Involve Staff

The more involved people feel, the less resistant to change they are. Include employees as early as possible in the process so they are *making* the change happen, not "being changed." Include everyone in the change process by making it easy and fun to participate. Create wacky contests for employees, and better yet, families of employees, to come up with creative ideas for the changes required. Hold a contest for the best change slogan. Set up special suggestion boxes and hold random draws from employees' valid suggestions to encourage people to contribute ideas on a regular basis. Create a fun voice-mail system to collect people's ideas about the change. For example, "If you feel the change the company is undertaking is, as Martha Stewart would say, a 'good thing,' please press #1 and tell us why. If you feel it's the stupidest idea since the pet rock, please press #2 and tell us why. Please be sure to yell clearly so we can capture all your brilliant ideas and suggestions."

④ Keep People Motivated

Change is stressful for people, so be patient and make an extra effort to keep morale high. Set up a special short-term morale booster squad. Hold a fun party or celebration ceremony partway through the change when folks really need a boost. Reward everyone with a SWAT team of masseuses, serve chocolate sundaes, order free pizzas or hire a stand up comedian to give everyone a good laugh when they most need it.

> *The fibers of resiliency are humor, creativity, persistence and optimism, and their roots reach well below the surface, ready to rise again and again when needed.*
>
> — Brian Luke Seaward, stress management author

The Humor Anchor

According to Gail Sheehy, author of PATHFINDERS, humor is one of four coping devices for dealing with change and uncertainty in our lives (the others she includes are prayer, dependency on work and friends). So when **you** can't find the obvious path through the "Forest of the Unknown," laugh a little and remember the words of Yogi Berra, "When you come to a fork in the road, take it."

REACTING TO CHANGE

If you are on the receiving end of change and feeling overwhelmed and under siege, practice accessing your humor resource through some of the techniques outlined in chapter 3. Take responsibility for how you react to the change going on around you. Remind yourself that regardless of the unknowns and the lack of control you feel, you are still in charge of your own emotions. Force yourself to look for what's good, and better yet, what strikes you funny about the change. Find a way to focus on the bright side by mentally reframing the situation. Try the old "The bad news is . . . but the good news is . . . " trick. Keep a humor first aid kit handy and access your humor as often as you need to. Double your portion of laugh breaks. And reward yourself with fun treats when things get extra stressful.

Finally, no matter how difficult things get during any massive change on the job, remember the words of M. Dale Baughman: "Humor is like a diaper change – it makes you feel comfortable for a while."

Humor, a "diaper change" for adults.

— *6* —

Humor as a Catalyst for Creativity

When in doubt, make a fool out of yourself. There is a microscopically thin line between being brilliantly creative and acting like the most gigantic idiot on earth. So what the hell, leap.

— Cynthia Heimel

There is an *exceptionally* strong link between creativity and humor. Mathematically, the humor as a creativity catalyst looks a little something like this:

Ha + Ha + Ha + Ha = AHA!

Although not as profound as $E=mc^2$, it's a lot easier to understand and a heck of a lot more fun. This link is obvious to anyone who has ever worked around a high-energy group of creative people or seen an innovative workplace in action. Humor and creativity are powerful forms of energy that feed off each other. So if you want to foster a more creative workplace culture, create an environment where play and humor are allowed to thrive. Let's look first at why this relationship is the perfect marriage.

Why Humor Leads to Brilliant New Ideas

Humor is by far the most significant activity of the human brain.

— Edward de Bono, creativity author

Just in case you need further justification for having more fun at the office, here are nine good reasons why fun, play and humor are such powerful catalysts for creativity.

① Creativity and Humor Involve Playing with Ideas and Changing Perspectives

Humor and creativity are about looking at the same thing as everyone else, but seeing something totally different. Both involve a derailment along a linear track of thought. Both involve making connections we normally wouldn't make. And both are about playing with existing ideas and concepts. As Lenore Terre, author of *Beyond Love and Work* suggests, "Play helps us avoid looking at problems head on, instead it forces us to come at them from somewhere off to the side."

It makes sense, then, that the more you play and flex your funny bone, the easier it becomes to make new connections and look at things from a fresh perspective. The creative brain, like anything else, requires exercise, and sharpening our sense of humor is one way to make sure the mass of neurons we lug around gets a regular workout.

Children seem to know this without being told, especially five-year-olds. One study suggests we peak creatively at around five. (Given this, I have a theory that five-year-olds could probably take over the world, except they can't because they don't know how to drive and aren't allowed out after dark.) That annoying phenomenon known as logic hasn't made itself completely at home in the five-year-old mind. Without hard and fast rules to channel them, children are masters at playing with their universe. To a child, a tree becomes a castle, the pet beagle is a fire breathing dragon and, yes, the sky really is green sometimes.

The bottom crayon line creatively is this—if you want to be

more creative, humor can help you tap into that five-year-old trapped inside and let him or her out to play for a while.

> *It is the child in the man that is the source of his uniqueness and creativeness, and the playground is the optimal milieu for the unfolding of his capacities and talents.*
> — Eric Hoffer

② Play Jump Starts the Brain

Have you ever suffered from mental constipation? I know I have. Here's how it works: you're in desperate need of a new idea so you sit down at a desk, place a blank sheet of paper in front of you, squint real hard and furrow your brow. You are certain the intense pain inside your skull will eventually lead to brilliant new ideas. Smoke pours out of your ears. Your body tenses up. You stare at the page. Half an hour later, you're sound asleep, curled up quietly across the top of your drool-covered notepad or keyboard. (By the way, you don't need to be alone to achieve this effect. Try gathering a bunch of like-minded individuals and stuffing them around a boardroom table on a hot afternoon, preferably after a big lunch. Dim the lights and turn on an overhead projector to achieve best results.)

In our awe of modern technology, we sometimes forget that we come preinstalled with the most amazing software you'll find anywhere—the human brain. According to one estimate, the human brain is capable of storing 20 million computer CDs worth of information. The problem is none of us arrived on the planet with a user manual. We walk around taking our own software for granted, yet we all recognize the need to boot up our computers, recharge our laptops, clean out our computer files and upgrade our computer systems every few years (or is it weeks now?).

Humor – the perfect way to jumpstart any brain

To get the best performance out of your brain's computing power, you need to recharge it, feed it, nourish it, stretch it, flex it and, every now and then, delete all those junk files floating around.

Play and humor will help you do just that. When you play, you develop new neural cells in areas devoted to memory and learning. Getting up out of your chair and engaging both your mind and body fires up those neurons. The simple act of standing up improves the flow of oxygen to the brain, as does laughter. Combine the two (movement and laughter) and your brain becomes more alert, fully charged and ready to go. In fact, as revealed in EEG data, laughter stimulates both hemispheres of the brain at the same time and may result in our brains operating at their highest capacity.

Film director Alfred Hitchcock recognized the need for a playful distraction during creative roadblocks. When screenwriters working with the legendary director became blocked, Hitchcock was known to interrupt them and regale them with long stories that had nothing to do with the script problem at hand. His strategy was bang on. After the mental change of focus, the writers would invariably get past the idea jam.

> *Play appears to allow our brains to exercise their very flexibility, to maintain and even perhaps renew the neural connections that embody our human potential to adapt, to meet any possible set of environmental conditions.*
> — Hara Estroff Marano

③ Play Reduces Inhibitions

Play and humor help reduce our inhibitions, which encourages us to share truly wild ideas in our workplace. If you've walked around flapping your arms like a chicken during a game of charades or pretended to be the first platypus on the moon during a theater improvisation exercise, you'll probably be a lot more at ease suggesting something totally novel. When we play, we feel no limitations. We become unaware of rules and ourselves. Play is a liberating experience that helps us tap into our creative energies.

> *Without playing with fantasy, no creative work has ever come to birth.*
> — C.G. Jung, Swiss psychologist

④ Play Helps Foster a Culture of Risk Taking

To foster a truly creative organization, you need to rock the boat, take risks and make mistakes. If you're not making mistakes, as the old saying goes, then chances are you're not doing anything new. *Smart* mistakes, after all, aren't mindless blunders, they're merely research and education.

Thomas Edison offered the perfect perspective on failure when he replied to a reporter's question about having failed to find a successful filament for the light bulb halfway through his experiments with: "I have not failed once. I have *succeeded* in finding 1500 ways *not* to make a light bulb."

Companies with a high fun quotient foster a culture that is supportive of risk takers. Perhaps it's the sense of adventure that accompanies play or the simple fact that to play and express our sense of humor involves taking a bit of risk and, sometimes, failing spectacularly. When we laugh, especially at our own pratfalls, we set a tone that says, "It's okay to screw up now and then. We aren't always perfect."

Humor not only helps people to take risks, it also encourages them to offer more creative ideas and to be *accepting* of creative ideas. Why? Because humor lets us play with a *representation* of reality, and experiment without any risk or fear of the consequences.

> *In a world continuously presenting unique challenges and ambiguity, play prepares us for an evolving planet.*
> — Robert Fagen

⑤ Humor and Creativity Challenge our Basic Assumptions

Humor's ability to derail routine tracks of thought and turn concepts on their head allows us to stand back from self-imposed rules and assumptions and examine our problems from a new perspective. Play and humor let us practice new ways of thinking and allow us to shuffle ideas and reorganize our thoughts. Humor jolts us into seeing things in a new way and prevents us from walking around on autopilot. And let's face it, there's no way we're going to come in for a creative landing when we're on autopilot.

> *If you obey all the rules, you miss all the fun.*
> — Katharine Hepburn

⑥ Humor Encourages Spontaneity

As most comedians will tell you, often the most effective humor is spontaneous. Spontaneity is also a key to brilliantly creative ideas, because it encourages you to express your ideas before your inner voice ("don't say that out loud, you'll sound foolish") censors them.

Play is a lost key. It unlocks the door to ourselves.
— Lenore Terre

⑦ Humor Helps Us Focus on Solutions Instead of Problems

Humor nudges us away from "blame-storming" (focusing on the problem and who's to blame) and into the world of brainstorming (focusing on solutions). Humor and play, by keeping us in a positive mood and an optimistic frame of mind, focus us on possibilities and block negative emotions that result in rigid thinking. And because humor and play are about changing perspectives and unleashing the mind, people can view workplace problems in a broader context and be reminded that, just maybe, a solution is possible for even the most overwhelming problems. Properly harnessed, humor shifts us away from convergent thinking, pushing aside the notion that there's only one answer or viewpoint and moving our minds into a "what if" frame of thinking, where the possibilities are limitless.

To be serious is to press for a specified conclusion. To be playful is to allow for unlimited possibility.
— James Carse

⑧ Humor Sends the Message: Creativity Wanted Here

If you want your customers to know that your organization truly values creativity and innovation, then taking a humorous approach to business can help reinforce that message. A company that does this is clearly saying to its customers: "We value ideas and creativity." It also sends the message to its employees that they work in a place where creative ideas are not only encouraged, but expected.

At the height of laughter, the universe is flung into a kaleidoscope of new possibilities.
— Jean Houston

9 Humor Can Help Sell Ideas

One of the most difficult parts of the creative process is selling and moving ideas through the labyrinth of a large bureaucracy. Humor, by fostering a more open, flexible and accepting environment, can ease the passage of any new ideas. Humor is also a powerful tool for selling new ideas and alleviating some of the apprehension staff or managers may have about accepting a new idea.

> *Humor is the only thing that keeps the human brain from turning into a raisin.*
>
> — Dan Piraro, *Bizarro* cartoonist

THE EXPERTS AGREE – HUMOR FUELS CREATIVITY

The University of Tel Aviv exposed high school students to a semester of humor studies (why didn't I have a high school like this?) and discovered the creativity of the students in the humor program soared substantially compared to other students. In another study, volunteers who watched humorous videos of comedians like Lily Tomlin were able to generate more creative ideas than people who didn't screen funny videos. According to Daniel Goleman, author of *Emotional Intelligence*, research shows that people put into good moods via humor are able to think through problems with more ingenuity. And a survey by 3M, reported in *Training Magazine*, found that two-thirds of all respondents listed play or humor as their favorite way of stimulating creativity in the workplace.

Yet another insightful study was reported in *What's So Funny? The Comic Conception of Culture and Society*, by Murray S. Davis. Davis gave subjects the task of solving a word anagram problem in small groups. Each group was to create as many different 4-letter words out of 10 scrambled letters as it could in a 10-minute period. The groups were analyzed based on the amount of joking and laughing in each group. The final score was as follows:

Level of Humor	Average Number of Words Generated
High-joking groups	75 words
Medium-joking groups	56 words
Low-joking groups	45 words

Psychologist Alice M. Isen from the University of Maryland offers the final thought on this matter: "Any joke that makes you feel good is likely to help you think more broadly and more creatively."

Unleashing the Creative Gremlins in Your Workplace

Beyond encouraging humor and play in the workplace, are there any concrete steps a workplace can take to foster a more creative atmosphere conducive to innovation? Some folks mistakenly believe that creativity is an elusive, mysterious phenomenon that can't possibly be "managed" in the traditional sense. Yet numerous workplaces dispel this misconception. You *can* create a work environment where creativity thrives on a regular basis. And it's just like planning for a romantic evening. Honest.

Imagine that tonight you are inviting someone special over and you want to send the message that romance is in the air. What would you do? If you're like me, you'd probably tackle this from a number of angles. First, I'd have a shower. Then I'd slip into something comfortable. Next, I'd take care of the physical ambience. Clean the place up. Dim the lights. Soft candles. Quiet jazz in the background. Fresh flowers. What about food and drink? Oysters, of course, and a fine bottle of wine. And when my mystery date arrived, would I complain about her tardiness or tell her I was recovering from some horrendous gastro-intestinal affliction? Of course not. I'd be an attentive listener. I'd probably compliment her. And if everything went according to plan, romance would ensue.

Can you imagine doing this *without* setting the stage properly? Of course not. That would be ridiculous. And yet that's the trap a lot of workplaces fall into when it comes to encouraging creativity. Too many organizations make the mistake of thinking all you need to do is tap people on the shoulder and say, "Go forth and spew brilliant ideas." It simply won't work. Particularly in a workplace where humor is suppressed, employees are demoralized, communication is poisoned and smart failures are punished. But, just like setting the stage for a romantic evening, by changing the workplace environment and culture, you truly can set the stage for inspiration.

STORMING THE BRAINS FOR IDEAS

The advertising world, and specifically ad man Alex Osborne, brought us the concept of brainstorming. The rules of brainstorming are simple: gather some folks (from 4 to 10 seems to be an ideal number) around a notepad, white board or flip chart, and fly at `er, shouting out as many ideas pertaining to a goal or problem as you can. It is crucial that there be no judging or blocking of anyone's ideas, *everything* is accepted. Brainstorming is about quantity over quality and leapfrogging off each other's suggestions to come up with new ideas. Naturally, this process leads to lots of ridiculous suggestions, but the point of the exercise is that you need to go through a process like this to get to idea #87, which just happens to contain the seed of something astoundingly brilliant. If you don't brainstorm, you might never get to idea #87 (by the way, I've patented idea #87, so don't even think about it). The effectiveness of brainstorming rests largely on one factor—the willingness of partici-pants to throw out truly wild ideas without fear of recrimination or embarrassment.

For workplaces that don't use an approach like this, brainstorm-ing can seem rather unorthodox. Like anything else, however, brainstorming is a skill you need to practice and train for. Once people get comfortable working with the process, brainstorming will quickly become second nature. To be truly effective, encourage potential brainstormers to keep the following guidelines in mind.

The 10 Creativity Commandments for an Effective Brainstorm

1. Gather 4 to 10 people (split larger groups into several smaller groups; if a group is too large, people may be less willing to con-tribute). And don't just gather like-minded people together, include people that don't know *anything* about the topic or even bring in clients who can offer a totally different perspective.

2. Meet in a relaxed, preferably fun location. In a *Training Magazine* survey, 90% of respondents reported that location had a signifi-cant impact on their creativity and 40% said their own work-space was the *least* conducive location for creativity. So remove any unwanted distractions, such as cell phones or computers, and replace them with *fun* distractions that might spark the group's creative energy, like props, toys or music. The best

choice for music, according to creativity experts, has no lyrics and limited mental demands on the listeners, such as classical, light jazz, or new age music.

3. Start with a fun icebreaker to loosen folks up. Brainstorming a few silly topics (uses for a paper clip or alternative titles to *Gilligan's Island*) or playing a theater improvisational game can help people get into the groove of the session and reduce inhibitions.

4. Assign a recorder or use a tape recorder to capture everyone's ideas. It's sometimes advantageous if the recorder does not participate in the brainstorm, so that the way ideas are captured isn't biased.

5. Write the issue or problem at the top of a flip chart or white board. Your issue or problem statement should be worded in a way that is not going to limit ideas or solutions. Make sure you're solving the right problem!

6. Set a time limit. Time pressure can force more spontaneity, a key ingredient in the formulation of truly innovative ideas. Anywhere from 5 to 15 minutes may be appropriate, depending on the scope of the issue. Remember, great ideas often come towards the end of a session.

7. Remind participants that there is no blocking of ideas, no judgments, no criticisms, no "buts" and no "that's the stupidest idea I ever heard."

8. Quantity rules—try to get as many ideas as you can.

9. Encourage participants to listen to each other's ideas, make new connections and leapfrog wildly off into uncharted waters.

10. Have fun! Use toys, noisemakers or goofy hats to instill a sense of play, enthusiasm and discovery in all of your brainstorming sessions. Get out of your seats and use your body to more fully engage your brain!

> *Your reasoning is silly, illogical and irrational . . .*
> *and it's beginning to make sense.*
> — Anon.

Child's Play?

Some child development experts suggest that rather than stuffing
children's heads and days with an endless stream of activities,
what children often need is to just kick back and play. Informal
play is what gives kids' minds a true workout, forcing them to use
their imagination and helping them to develop their thinking skills
in a whole range of different situations. The question of the day
is, why would this advice apply only to children? It shouldn't. As
Brian Sutton-Smith, a professor of psychology at the University of
Pennsylvania, reported in PSYCHOLOGY TODAY, when adults play
their memory is better, they are cognitively more capable and
they are happier. It sure doesn't sound like child's play to me.

Child's Play – Part II

The BrainStore, a creative consulting company based in Biel,
Switzerland, regularly taps into the minds of young people when
looking for new ideas. Their Brain Net is a 1,500-person computer network made up of mostly 13- to 20-year-olds that helps
feed new trends and ideas to the BrainStore. When working with
clients, the professional staff of the BrainStore teams up with
young people as a way of tapping into the imagination and
enthusiasm of children. This is another reminder that if you can't
bring children to your workplace, you need to at least tap into
that child-like attitude as often as you can.

DILBERT reprinted by permission of United Feature Syndicate, Inc.

COMMUNICATING FOR CREATIVITY

How you communicate in a workplace can have a huge impact on the creative process. You can foster a style of communication that supports and encourages each other's ideas, or, more typical of many workplaces, you can excel at destroying each other's ideas through the power of the words you use. I'll always remember the time I excitedly suggested what I thought to be the most brilliant idea of the century (if not the millennium), only to have a senior manager peer over his glasses in a rather Scrooge-like manner and ask me, "If it's such a great idea, why isn't someone else doing it?"

Charles "Chic" Thompson, author of *What a Great Idea!*, calls these "killer phrases." We've all heard them and we've all likely used them—phrases, words or body language that function like heat-seeking missiles. The target of these missiles? Ideas. When someone lobs out a truly innovative, never-before-heard idea we fire off one of these idea busters, ensuring that the person who suggested the idea beats a hasty retreat and never dares bring forward a new idea again in our presence. Not only do idea busters reduce people's morale by making them feel that their contributions don't merit serious consideration, they also demolish seeds of new ideas before they're given any chance of survival.

Ideas are as fragile as newborn babies. They need time to nourish and develop into fully grown concepts capable of striking out on their own. It takes only one sarcastic or derisive comment to kill these fledgling ideas faster than a speeding bullet. And often we are our own worst enemy. Most of us censor our own ideas with "inner speak" before we get them out of our mouth. So it's tough enough getting a new idea past our own insecurities and fears without having a roomful of vultures ready to pounce on them.

Now don't get me wrong – there *are* bad ideas out there (I just watched the sequel to *Saturday Night Fever* while holed up in a hotel room, so I know they exist). In fact, there are downright horrible, stupid and even dangerous ideas that never should see the light of day. So of course, there is a point in the creative process when ideas need to be analyzed, critiqued, and modified or reshaped before they come to fruition. However, too many brilliant ideas end up dead on the cutting-room floor because we never give them a sporting chance.

Fortunately humor rides to the rescue once again. Workplaces with high levels of fun and positive morale foster greater cooperation and flexible thinking, so people are less likely to shoot down each other's ideas. And, humorous techniques can be used to remind people to avoid these idea busters and encourage more positive dialogue.

The first step to banishing idea busters is to identify the more common ones used in your workplace. Hold a fun brainstorming session or contest to see who can come up with the most idea-busting phrases, circulate the list to staff and post it in your meeting rooms as a reminder to avoid these phrases at all costs. Then, penalize people who utter idea busters, for example, have violators pay a 25-cent fine into the coffee fund, squirt them with water pistols or make them don a silly costume item (like a "bonehead hat") each time they're found guilty of uttering a "we've always done it this way" sort of phrase.

Here's just a small sample of some commonly used idea busters.

Verbal Idea Busters (a.k.a. "VIBs")

We tried it before (in 1917)	What have you been smoking?
It'll never work	Yes, but . . .*
There's no time!	There's no money!
Are you nuts?	But, we've always done it this way!
No	Someone else tried it and it didn't work
If it ain't broke . . .	It's not practical
Let's keep to what works	We don't pay you to think
Let's form a committee!	Let's wait until our competition starts doing it
Yeah, right!	We'll never get approval
Are you serious?	You can't be serious!
You're kidding, right?	If it's such a great idea, why isn't someone else doing it?

*"But" is simply a clever way of saying NO! Its overuse in the workplace leads to "but-headed thinking" and should be avoided at all costs.

Non-verbal Idea Squashers—Silent But Deadly

Silence	Leaving the room
Smirking	Laughing
Rolling eyes	Folding arms across the chest
Sighing	Dropping the head dramatically to the chest
Furrowing of the brow	Staring out the window looking for a sign from God
Head shaking	Burying face in hands
Looking at the floor	Looking at the ceiling

The man with an original idea is a crank until the idea succeeds.

— Mark Twain

FAMOUS IDEA SQUASHERS FROM HISTORY

Great spirits have always encountered violent opposition from mediocre minds.

— Albert Einstein

There are two types of people, those who *make things happen* (often in the face of everyone telling them that their idea or plans will never work) and those who try to *stop* things from happening. These latter folks are so busy pointing out why our dreams or ideas will never work that they don't get around to creating their own. The next time you feel compelled to shoot down someone's idea or dream, keep in mind the following quotes, and ask yourself: Which side of the quote would I prefer to be on?

"You'll *never* make it. Go back to Liverpool."
As told to the Beatles by an American record executive in 1962

"Heavier than air flying machines are impossible."
Lord Kelvin, chemist, in 1885

"What use would this company make of this electric toy."
Carl Orton, president of Western Union, speaking to Alexander Graham Bell

"Star Trek will never fly because it's too expensive."
Television executive rejecting the first Star Trek series

"You will never make a career as an actor."
As told to Harrison Ford by a movie director after his first bit part

"Who the hell wants to hear actors talk?"
Harry M. Warner, Warner Brothers Pictures, 1927

"The horse is here to stay, but the automobile is only a passing fad."
*Bank president advising his nephew not to invest in the
Ford Motor Company in 1893*

"Face it, Civil War pictures have never made a dime."
*MGM producer advising his boss against buying the rights to
Gone With the Wind*

"People will get tired of staring at a plywood box every night."
Movie mogul Daryl Zanuck, on the threat of television, in 1946

"High speed rail travel is impossible because people will suffocate."
Dr. Dionysius Lardner

"Everything that can be invented has been invented."
*Charles H. Duell, Commissioner of the U.S. Patent Office,
recommending the closure of the patent office in 1899*

IDEA SUPPORTERS

The flip side of banning idea-busting language is to foster a climate where people support each other's ideas. We need to encourage Idea Supporting Phrases ("ISPs") like the following (if you've never heard these expressions in your workplace, practice saying them in the mirror to get used to what they sound like):

Yes and . . .!	What do we need to do to make this idea work?
Let's try it and see!	How can I help?
Great! And here's how we can make it work even better!	What obstacles are in the way, and how can we remove them?
Does the Nobel Peace Prize committee know about you?	Let's give it a try for six months!

Wow!	What a great idea! Why didn't I think of that?
You might be onto something!	It just might be crazy enough to work!
We'll be the first to try this!	We'll be pioneers!
How can we reduce the risk?	How we can nourish this idea and help it grow into something truly beautiful and exciting?

Humor and creativity are kissing cousins. If you want to develop your creativity invite more humor into your life – and vice versa.
— Dr. Joel Goodman, director of The Humor Project

CHANGE YOUR VIEWPOINT!

Since both humor and creativity involve viewing situations or potential problems from a changed perspective, it should be no surprise that some of the techniques you can use to generate ideas are also great sources of humor.

Brainstorm the opposite of the problem. Looking at a situation in reverse or backwards is a common source of humor. For example, Henny Youngman had a classic joke about how some beautiful showgirls had a dressing room next door to his. One day he discovered a hole in the wall between the two rooms. "It's okay," he quipped, "I let them look." Humor like this, called "reverse logic" by comics, creates laughter by switching our perspective on a situation.

Brainstorming the opposite perspective is also a simple way to generate new ideas. If you're trying to figure out ways to motivate employees, brainstorm how to *de-motivate* them. Brainstorm what would happen if you *increased* costs or what might happen if your customers sold to you? Or set out to write the *worst* possible set of instructions or press release you can. Not only will this generate some laughter, but the changed perspective can lead to new ideas you might have missed while looking at the problem head on.

Exaggerate a characteristic. Exaggeration is a classic form of humor, and another technique that forces you to look at a situation in a new light. What ideas might you develop if you wildly exaggerated some characteristic associated with the problem or issue?

Left Brained or Right?

We tend to think of highly creative people as being "right brain" thinkers. The reality is that to be creative or to use humor effectively we use both sides of our brain. Although the right side may help us with the occasional flash of brilliance, we need our logical left side to analyze, judge, critique and sell our ideas in the workplace. And to "get" a joke, we need both sides of our brain to understand the logic that is broken by the incongruity in the punchline.

The Laughing Defense

Brainwashing and brainstorming are polar opposites. Brainwashing involves mental manipulation that reduces a person's mental flexibility and ability to think clearly. Research into brainwashing techniques has discovered that humor is one of the most powerful weapons to combat brainwashing. If a subject laughs while being brainwashed, the brainwashing process must start over from the very beginning. This sounds like further proof that a creative, flexible mind is highly dependent on a healthy sense of humor.

Look at the situation from the perspective of another profession or person. We saw in chapter 3 how mentally reframing a stressful situation helps us find humor. Reframing by stepping into someone else's shoes is also a way to find new ideas because it forces us to take on new perspectives. For example, how would Robin Williams, Miss Piggy or a basketball coach improve staff morale in your workplace? How would a plumber view your advertising dilemma? What would a chef see in your budget-cutting challenge?

Random association. Humor and creativity are often born out of purely random, sometimes accidental, associations that ordinarily wouldn't make any sense. Random associations during brainstorming is yet another way to force new connections. A simple way to do this is to draw a word from a dictionary or from a bag of magnetic poetry and then examine your problem using the word as a trigger.

For example, what marketing ideas are you led to by thinking about an alligator? A horseshoe? The color purple? Imagination? Celery? Campbell's Chunky Soup was born using this method. The random word "handle" led to "utensil," which led to "fork," which led to the famous ad tag line, "The soup so chunky you can eat it with a fork."

At the creative agency Play, a chalkboard is used to capture random ideas. Employees write down a word related to a problem or goal they are working on, then staff add ideas to the chalkboard as they stroll by.

Ask questions. Humorists and creative people share a common trait— curiosity. It may have killed the cat, but it's a sure-fire way to magnify your humor lens *and* find new ideas. The key is simply forcing yourself to ask *lots* of questions and *different* questions relating to a problem. Playing detective or investigative journalist compels you to examine an issue from as many angles as possible. What if we . . .? How come there isn't . . .? Why can't we just . . .? Why do people . . .? How can we . . .? You can't truly come up with a new idea unless you force yourself to look at the problem from a different viewpoint, and the easiest way to do this is to ask a different question.

> *When you ask a dumb question – you get a smart answer.*
> — Aristotle

WORKING AT PLAY – CREATIVITY IN ACTION

A company famous for its inspiring workplace culture and its ability to generate ideas is the creative agency Play. It epitomizes the essence of play and creativity we've explored throughout this chapter. Its physical environment is definitely playful—Polaroid photos line one wall, and bright colors, magazines, toys, trampolines and containers of Play Doh (which are handed out upon arrival) are the norm at its office in Richmond, Virginia.

Play's workplace culture and attitudes match the physical playfulness of the surroundings. When I sat down out on the front sidewalk with three members of the Play team on a sunny day in Virginia, I instantly thought to myself, "This company would be great to work for." As we talked about humor, creativity and the universe, other staff members came and went, carrying Hula Hoops, gigantic rubber balls and assorted other tools of their trade. The workplace bubbled over with energy, yet at the same time had a relaxed, comfortable atmosphere about it.

We focused our discussion around the following question: "What is the key to the internal creativity here, and how does the company foster that same climate in its clients?" There was of course no single answer. What became clear, however, was that the company nurtured a playful and energetic attitude in everything it did. From banging a drum to announce meetings, to storytelling time, to their Friday 5:00 p.m. toasts to celebrate victories in the past week, it was clear that humor and creativity were the normal modus operandi. The combination of workplace rituals and wacky surroundings created a feeling or atmosphere known internally as "Mojo." If you want to be continually creative, they say, you've got to have Mojo.

Using toys, outlandish games and brain-stretching exercises (such as relating kindergarten quotes to everyday business problems), the Play team tries to infuse other workplaces with this same Mojo. To create Mojo, the team holds brainstorming sessions that include a mixed bag of staff from a client's company in order to include as many different perspectives as possible. The real key to unleashing creativity in organizations according to the Play team: it's giving people permission to play and encouraging people to be themselves. At Play, they have those rules down to a fine art.

CLOSING THOUGHTS – THE FINAL AHA!

The creative mind is a playful mind; the creative organization is a playful organization. So if you want to be more innovative and creative, don't *just* plan for humor during your next brainstorming session. Invite humor into your work lives on a regular basis and, then, get out of the way and start clearing out some space. You'll need to make room for all those brilliant new ideas!

— 1 —

Motivating the Troops Through Laughter

If you are working in a company that is not enthu-
siastic, energetic, creative, clever, curious and just
plain fun, you've got troubles, serious troubles.
— Tom Peters, management guru

There are two ways to approach work, as illustrated by how we face the ultimate work-attitude litmus test—Monday mornings.

Option 1: You wake up at 6:30 a.m. and your first thought is a simple one: "Oh, God, it's Monday." Your hair looks like you barely survived Hurricane Hazel. You roll onto the family dog, stagger to the bathroom and give yourself a quick sponge bath with a damp piece of toilet paper. You get dressed into your "regulation prison wear"— ties for the men, pantyhose for the women (and, let's be honest, for *some* of the men). Paramedics greet you in the kitchen to start a caffeine IV drip (there's no way you're going to work unless you're heavily drugged). You crawl into your sedan and cruise to work on autopilot, steering with your forehead while holding an espresso precariously between your thighs. You walk into the office in a zombie-like manner, staring straight ahead as you pass co-workers in the hallway. There's no eye contact. No one speaks. You've decided that work is like war. You'll just go in, do your job, hope you survive until Friday and get out. Your first goal is to make it to Wednesday. Hump day. Because you know from atop the hump, you can see your ultimate destination – the weekend. And if you can just muster up the strength to crawl across the finish line at 4:30 on Friday afternoon, you know you'll be released on your own recognizance for good behavior. One week finished. One week closer to death.

> *Humans are creative, fun and inquiring, yet work*
> *for so many is monotonous, complex and dreary.*
> — Andy Law

Option 2: You wake up at 6:30 a.m. and the theme from *Rocky* fills the air. You leap out of bed like a Jack-in-the-Box on too much Viagra. You passionately kiss your spouse. You passionately kiss your dog. You dance naked in front of the mirror. Why? Because it's Monday morning, the start of your work week! You cartwheel into the shower and sing operatic love songs as you think about the week ahead. You're so pumped that after leaving the shower, you don't bother toweling off; instead, you run around the house naked, air drying yourself. You get dressed and check your hair—not a single hair out of place. Grabbing your briefcase, you declare triumphantly that you're not driving into work, you're running into work! And you're off! You run down the median of the freeway, leap over fences and sail over paperboys, high-fiving people as you close in on the office. You soar into your office, vault onto your desk and punch your fist into the air, while the theme from *Rocky* rises again. Why? Because it's Monday. And you realized long ago that waking up on a Monday morning to go to work . . . is a really, really good thing (given the alternative). And because you've decided that no matter what is going on at work, this is the attitude you will take to work each and every day.

> *Our attitude is the crayon that colors the world.*
> — Allen Klein

Okay, quiz time. Which category would you prefer to fall into, option 1 or option 2? Better yet, which group would you like your co-workers to fall into? (I know some of you are thinking, "Isn't there something in between these two nut cases?")

Adding more humor to your work life is not likely going to turn you into a hyperactive, outgoing, pumped-up cheerleader. But if you don't relish the idea of being trapped in the "Night of the Living Dead Office" scenario, then adding fun and humor to your work on an ongoing basis is certainly a step in the right direction.

Some people might wonder which comes first, high morale or lots of fun? Don't you, after all, need high morale *in order* to have lots of fun? Humor and morale are as intricately linked as the chicken and the egg: when morale is high, it's easier to make people laugh. Conversely, when people laugh a lot, morale improves. It's a not-so-vicious cycle that creates a simple formula for workplace success.

> *Age may wrinkle the face, but lack of enthusiasm*
> *wrinkles the soul.*
> — Samuel Ullman

The pinnacle of the human race?

Oh God, It's Monday!

Monday mornings are a peak time for heart attacks, suicides, strokes, automobile accidents and absenteeism. This sounds like a "Monday morning wake-up call" that major changes are needed in many of our work environments to move people away from OGIM ("Oh God, It's Monday") to TGIM ("Thank God, It's Monday!")!

> *Wanting to work is so rare a want that it should be*
> *encouraged.*
> — Abraham Lincoln

WHAT'S MY MOTIVATION?

What motivates people to work harder, be a better team player or be more enthusiastic on the job? Although there is no definitive answer, there are a few basic truths.

1. To each his or her own. Different people have different motivators, so be careful about painting everyone with the same motivational brush. Managers need to connect at the individual level and build relationships one person at a time. If you want to find out what motivates your co-workers or employees, here's a little tip. ASK THEM!

2. Intrinsic (internal) motivators are more poweful than external motivators. Some argue it's impossible to motivate anyone, except yourself. Although there's some truth to this, workplace culture clearly has a huge impact on morale and motivation levels. Organizations need to create the type of culture that supports and frees up people's intrinsic motivators.

3. You get what you reward. It's a cliché because it's true. Animal trainers know this. The trainers at Sea World describe their technique for training everything from seals to killer whales as a two-step process. First, they build a relationship based on trust. Second, they reward positive behavior. If it works for seals, maybe it works for people too.

4. Money is not a great motivator. Yes, there are people who will do nearly anything for a buck and there are others struggling to make ends meet who will naturally view money as their primary motivation for getting up on a Monday morning. Financial rewards, however, are found to have only a short-term effect on most people. Remember that money is an exchange for work done—it gets people to show up. But if you want to move people out of the rat race and into the human race, you need to think seriously about improving the quality of their work lives and touching people where it counts, in their heart.

5. Motivation isn't a one-time event. Or even a two, three or six times a year event. As Zsa Zsa Gabor said, "Husbands are like fires. They go out if unattended." The same thing is true of employees. To keep employees (or ourselves!) burning with passion, we need to continually add fuel, stoke the fires and create some sparks.

6. It's little things that count. Studies have shown that even huge, potentially life-altering events (positive or negative) tend to have little impact on a person's overall outlook or happiness a year or two after the event. Instead of the swimming pool, the trip around the world or that hefty raise, researchers have found that our basic level of happiness is influenced more by small things we experience on a daily basis, like reading a good book, savoring a good cup of coffee, walking the dog and laughing with close friends. So small gestures done on a regular basis in the workplace can have huge payoffs.

7. Low morale is a symptom of a problem. Low morale happens for any number of reasons, ranging from a lack of employee recognition to poor communications or incompetent leadership. To add humor and passion to the workplace, you need to focus on fixing the root cause of low morale and treat the entire patient, not just the symptoms. Humor, when administered properly, helps treat both the symptoms *and* the patient.

People who feel good about themselves produce good results.

— Ken Blanchard

Is Work Really a Four-Letter Word?

Language shapes perception. How we label things influences the filter we see them through. So if you feel like you cough up a hair-ball every time you say the word "work," it's likely that much tougher to get excited about what you do. It could be worse, though. The Spanish word for work, trabajo, comes from a Latin word meaning an instrument of torture, while the Irish term "job" has a double meaning of a temporary work assignment and excrement. The root of the term "labor" in many languages means "compulsory drudgery to keep alive." Gee, "work" is sounding better and better all the time.

I love my job, it's the work I hate.

— Winston Churchill

Thanks a Lot!—
Creating an Enthusiastic Work Environment

To love what you do and feel that something matters – what could be more fun?

— Katherine Graham

We know that financial rewards aren't strong motivators, so what exactly *does* motivate the average Joe or Joe-Ann? Many surveys, including my own, have suggested some of the strongest workplace motivators are:

🍄 Thanks. A simple and sincere thanks for a job well done.

🍄 Recognition of a person's contribution or ideas (even when they aren't used!) and of the person's value to an organization.

🍄 Being able to contribute in a meaningful way. Increasingly, people want to know their work counts for something, that they make a difference in a positive way and are making the best use of their creative energy. More than ever, people are looking for real meaning in their work.

These three motivators overlap to a great degree. Many people, see being given assignments that are challenging and meaningful, as a form of recognition and thanks. The great news is that none of these motivators involve rocket science and none take a Herculean effort to achieve. The challenge is that because most of these things are easy and simple to do, they are also easy not to do.

Highly energized and passionate workplaces require a workplace climate where thanking each other is second nature, a task that can't be left to managers alone, because some won't get around to it in this millennium. Recognition in the workplace works best when it's a shared responsibility among everyone. And for praise to be most effective, it must be sincere (don't overdo it or it becomes meaningless), specific (tied to an observable behavior), timely and 100% positive. If you thank someone for staying at the office until midnight and then add, "Oh, by the way, next time could you . . .," the folks being praised tend to remember only the part where the other shoe dropped. So leave any corrective feedback for another discussion. When you want to say thanks, just say thanks.

Successful organizations and individuals also know that one of the keys to success is to celebrate milestones along the journey. The more you celebrate the small steps, the faster you reach the big goals and the more goals you accomplish. So create an atmosphere of *continual* celebration and excitement. Just be careful—enthusiasm is highly contagious!

One last element of a successful and highly motivated workforce is that elusive animal known as "teamwork." Organizations pay an abundance of lip service to the importance of teamwork, yet few make a concerted effort to do anything about it. Although having clear goals and a well-defined vision are necessary for creating well-oiled teams, organizations also need to create opportunities for employees to get to know each other at a human level. You don't have to like your co-workers, but you do need to work alongside them. Fun activities and workplace humor are great ways to break down professional barriers. The more we know and understand the human being behind the position, the easier it is to appreciate, respect and understand the real person lurking inside.

Humor is a natural ingredient in a highly successful team. Laughter is, after all, a highly social activity. As Robert Provine reported in *American Scientist* magazine, people are 30 times more likely to laugh with other people than when alone. Humor makes us more flexible, less defensive, more open and more approachable – in other words, an ideal "team player." And as a University of Israel study showed, 70% of good marriages depend heavily on a healthy sense of humor. If humor can help hold marriages together, undoubtedly it can help hold teams together in the workplace.

In short, humor is a powerful human connector, and an effective way to say thanks, celebrate in a memorable way and help workers get to know each other at a more human (and *humane*) level.

> *Dozens of companies are finding that employees*
> *who laugh together, stay together, produce more,*
> *invent more and work more cohesively as a team.*
> — Bradford Swift

WHO'S YOUR CHIEF IMAGINATION OFFICER?

To create an atmosphere of fun and enthusiasm in the workplace, start with the basics, like what we call ourselves. How would you like your business card and stationary to announce your job title as "Chief Imagination Officer"? Or how about the "VP of Cool"? The "Princess of Persuasion"? These are actual job titles, many of them featured in *Fast Company* magazine's regular feature, "Job Titles of the Future." Now some of you may be thinking, "What's in a name?" Actually, quite a bit. Our job titles are highly visible labels we tote around everyday so creating job titles that evoke enthusiasm and stir the imagination might make it a tad easier to get excited about our jobs. Developing inspirational or fun job titles also sends the message that you are a company where creativity and innovation is a way of life. As an added bonus, offbeat titles create a more memorable impression with clients, one that will help distinguish you from the rest of the pack.

If you can't change your job title, then at least establish a "nickname title" that captures the true spirit of your job, your personal voice and the *real* role you perform in the organization. You can slip this underneath your formal title, for example, Hank Sputnik, Manager of Human Resources, a.k.a. The Wizard of Oz. You could also link this to a contest for the most creative job title on staff.

At the creative agency Play, each staff member has a unique job title inspired by a group brainstorm, with the employee having final veto power on any decision. One employee I met had the job title "Flying Buttress," which he chose because it represents "style and form" – two qualities he saw as an essential part of his personality and function in the company. At Metrographics in Calgary, Alberta, employees also have wacky job titles, including "Jedi Knight," "Cement Shoes" and "Design Diva."

Here are a few more real-life examples:

Troublemaker	Minister of Enlightenment
Director of Mind and Mood	Gatekeeper
Project Guru	Internet Evangelist
Notionologist	The Quarterback
Young Gun	Human Being
Master of Mischief	Creatologist
Director of Fun	Vibe Evolver
Rocketman	Minister of Comedy
Chief Entertainment Officer (CEO)	

Not only are these job titles fun and inspirational, but the jobs that go with them reflect how organizations are starting to focus on the creative, human and fun side of business. The "Director of Fun," for example, works at Sprint Paranet. Her job is to help create a fun, stable and supportive work environment for the 1,200 employees in her company. The Human Being works for the Coffee People company; her job title reflects her commitment to customer service and putting people first. In fact, these job titles have inspired me so much I'm changing my own. From here on, I'm going by the official title: "Professional Giggle-O."

POTENTIAL CAUSES/EXCUSES FOR CELEBRATION

So you've bought into the idea of celebrating more often to raise your workplace spirit, but you don't know what or when to celebrate? Don't worry, there's always March 26th, a.k.a. "Make Your Own Holiday Day." If you want a better reason to celebrate, check out these possibilities. And above all else, don't forget to celebrate April 1st, which many folks are trying to formally recognize as the official Fun at Work Day.

General Possibilities (not tied to any specific date)
Employee birthdays
Team birthdays (group celebration once a month for all birthdays within the month)
Employee anniversary dates (dates employees started with the company)
Company anniversaries (the date the company was founded)
Fiscal New Year's Eve (New Year's Eve party on the start of your company's new fiscal year)
Completion of major projects
Winning contracts
Record attendance
New recruits day (depending on the number, hold once a month or twice a year)
Employee reunion day
Promotions day (celebrate anyone whose received a promotion in the last six months)
Job swap day (swap jobs for a day to walk a mile in a co-worker's shoes)
Take your family/kids/parents or pet to work day
Family open house day
Customer open house day
Customer appreciation day
(name of employee) day or week

Specific Dates Worthy of Celebration
These include some dates you likely didn't know existed. I've listed some wacky ones in case there's some connection to your particular company or profession.
New Year's Eve/Day

Human Resources Month (January, United States)
Clean Off Your Desk Day, January 13
National Hat Day, January 18
Groundhog Day, February 2
Valentine's Day, February 14
Employee Appreciation Day, March 10
St. Patrick's Day, March 17
Make Your Own Holiday Day, March 26
Easter
April Fool's Day, April 1
Humor Month (April)
Publicity Stunt Week, April 1 - 7 (United States)
Volunteer Week, April 9 - 15
Administrative Professionals Day, April 24
Administrative Professionals Week (starting 3rd Sunday of April)
Earth Day, April 20
Take Your Child to Work Day, April 27
World Laughter Day, first Sunday in May
International Nurses Day, May 12
Barbecue Month, May
National Receptionists' Day, May 9
National Hug Day, June 12 (United States)
Take Your Pet to Work Week, June 18 - 24
Canada Day, July 1
Independence Day, July 4 (United States)
Anti-Boredom, Hot Dog, Ice Cream and Picnic Month all in July
National Ice Cream Day (3rd Sunday in July) (United Sates)
National Smile Week, 1 week of August
National Clown Week, 1 week of August
International Lefthanders Day, August 13
Joke Day, August 16 (United States)
National Relaxation Day, August 15
Take Your Teddy Bear to Work Day, October 11
Train Your Brain Day, October 13
Canadian Thanksgiving (2nd Monday of October)
Boss Day, October 16
Halloween, October 31
Hello Day, November 21 (say hello to 10 new people)
Slinkie Day, November 24
American Thanksgiving (last Thursday in November)
Christmas Season

Boss Day

Boss Day was first declared in 1958, when bosses were real bosses (and real bossy). It began when Ms. Haroski, a secretary with State Farm Insurance in Illinois, bought her boss lunch the first year on the job because he was just so darned nice. She chose October 16 because that was her father's birthday. The tribute caught on. In 1998, Boss Day generated almost $1 million (U.S.) in card sales. According to Hallmark, Boss Day cards ranked 18th out of 20 card days that year, beating out Nurses Day and April Fool's Day. (Among the recipients on Boss Day was U.S. President Bill Clinton who received a hand-written poem from Monica Lewinsky.)

Bring Your Parents to Work Day?

In November 1999, the New York offices of Organic, a web design and computer services company, invited employees' parents to spend half a day learning what their offspring actually do with their lives. Close to 125 parents ate pizza and learned more about their children's careers than they ever could have imagined.

AND THE WINNER IS . . .

Fun award ceremonies (or adding some fun to your regular awards nights) can provide a much-needed diversion during the middle of a busy period or a great "end of season" celebration. You can ham things up by spoofing the Oscars, and dole out individual or team awards that are fun, yet still encourage appropriate behavior. Southwest Airlines hands out "Heart and Soul," "Creativity and Guts" and "Tell It Like It Is" awards to its employees. Hershey Foods has the "Exalted Order of the Extended Neck" for anyone who sticks their neck out and takes a smart risk.

Any job worth doing is worth celebrating and rewarding. In 1999, the first-ever "Zamboni Driver of the Year" award was handed out through the National Hockey League. And some bill collectors have a "Now I've Heard It All" award, given to whoever has heard the best excuse for why someone can't pay their bill. The prize, naturally, is a trophy of a bull rider.

Curtis Armstrong Week

The 1980's television series Moonlighting, starring Bruce Willis and Cybill Shepherd, was not, by all accounts, a very happy work environment. Near the end of its run, Bruce Willis decided the entire cast and crew needed a little injection of fun. Willis devised "Curtis Armstrong Week" – a wacky tribute to the star that played his goofy sidekick. The celebrations included a parade, band and the usual assortment of funny tribute speeches. Although the festivities interrupted shooting of an episode, it helped raise everyone's spirit with a much-needed injection of fun. So why not hold your own "Curtis Armstrong Week"? It doesn't have to be as outlandish, but all employees could have their own week (or at least their own day) designated throughout the year when they receive a few extra little perks, like a welcome-to-work banner, free office coffee for the week, their car washed by co-workers and an afternoon off.

There are no menial jobs, just menial attitudes.
— William J. Beaumont

The possibilities for fun awards are endless.

Best Sense of Humor	Best Answering Machine Message
Nicest Smile	Most Succinct Memo Writer
Iron Person Award (for best attendance)	Most Memorable Blooper
Rookie of the Year	Friendliest Phone Voice
Most Creative Idea	Most Fun Department
Most Creative Excuse Award	Foot-in-Mouth Award
Most Technologically Challenged	Sexiest Phone Voice
Most Likely to OD on Coffee	Most Likely to Staple Themselves
Wackiest Tie Collection	Most Likely to Jam the Photocopier
The Oscar (for the messiest desk/office)	The Felix (for the tidiest desk/office)
The Person Least Likely to . . .	The Person Most Likely to . . .

The Person-Who-Comes-Closest-To-Violating-the-Dress-Code Award

The employer generally gets the employees they deserve.
— Sir Walter Bibey

What to Get, What to Get?

Here are just a few suggestions for rewards, awards or perks for employees.

Free coffee	Mention in newsletter	Afternoon off
Chocolate treats	Car wash	Video rental coupons
Movie tickets	Cafeteria dish/office floor named in their honor	
Museum tickets	Meaningful job titles	T-shirts
Training course of their choice		Sporting events tickets
Free massage	Flowers	Stress squeeze balls
Chocolate sundaes	Mention in newspaper	Profile in newsletter
Wall of Fame inclusion	Cartoon books	Work-related books
Magazine subscriptions	Humorous books	This book
One of my other books	Manicure	Wacky toys
Home pick up in a limo	Theater tickets	Dinner reservations

MOTIVATION MANIA –
IDEAS TO WORK AND LAUGH BY

Laughter is aerobic exercise for the spirit.
— Bob Czimbal

There's certainly no shortage of fun ways to say thanks, to celebrate or to add positive energy to your workplace. The following ideas and examples have worked successfully in businesses throughout North America. Not all of them fall directly under the heading of "humor," but for humor in the workplace to flourish, you need to create a culture where activities and celebrations like these become second nature.

🍄 Say thanks with simple, small and fun rewards. According to Bob Nelson, author of *1,001 Ways to Reward Employees*, people should shoot for a ratio of four positive strokes for every negative comment. Chocolate treats, free coffee, donuts or wacky office toys are simple ways of saying thanks with a lighter touch. Tape Hershey Kisses, small packages of M & M's or mini chocolate bars to memos or thank you cards. Harry V. Quadracci, president of Quad/Graphics has delivered Popsicles to workers on the plant floor during heat waves via a tricycle. And at AIT Corporation in Ottawa, employees receive chocolates with motivational messages inside them each week.

🍄 Deliver a rousing standing ovation to workers just for making it into the office on Monday morning.

🍄 Give fun awards to folks who make it through tough times. Allen Klein, in his wonderful book *The Courage to Laugh*, describes the Golden Casket Award given to the staff of a hospice after they worked through a particularly tough night shift.

🍄 Keep a stock of humorous thank you cards in your desk to make it as easy as possible to write thank you notes. Sound cards are also available that applaud or actually say "thanks."

🍄 Have a prize for the best team or department name or slogan.

🍄 Have managers wash employees' cars, serve refreshments, dish lunch or scoop chocolate sundaes during a busy time for frontline employees.

🍄 Create your own "Hall/Wall of Fame." Why should music stars and sports celebrities be the only ones to get indoctrinated into a hall of fame? Create your own with fun photos and creative titles like "Rookie of the Year." The Nike Store in Eugene, Oregon, has a Heritage Wall which includes the first shoe molds that founder Bill Bowerman made with his waffle iron. Southwest Airlines headquarters has walls lined with awards, cards and employee photos.

☂ Create an office yearbook or photo album that celebrates and acknowledges employee accomplishments, both professional and personal. Include fun photos, memorable speeches, blooper lists, fun awards, top-10 lists, etc. Have employees sign it the way they would a high school yearbook.

☂ Celebrate birthdays and significant milestones in employees' personal lives. If you have a large staff, then hold a once-per-month birthday celebration that pays tribute to anyone having a birthday during that month.

☂ Celebrate small victories. Some sales companies have rituals where employees ring a bell every time a sale is made. At a Utah plant that manufactures booster rockets for the space shuttle, employees can make paper airplanes when they've achieved their quotas. At Schiff, Hardin and Waite, a Chicago-based law firm, new associates who pass the bar exam are rewarded with "edible applause" in the guise of hand-shaped popcorn treats.

☂ Celebrate your company's significant dates, such as the founding anniversary date.

☂ Celebrate the anniversary dates of when employees started working with the organization. Momentum Business Systems sends employees on short paid vacations when they reach a significant anniversary date.

☂ Create a celebrations and social activities calendar.

☂ Hold a "match the employee to the baby picture" contest.

☂ Hold a "match the employee to their pet" contest.

☂ Hold an employee scavenger hunt, where employees have one week to find co-workers who match certain personal characteristics (e.g., find someone who flys model airplanes on the weekend, someone who owns a weasel ranch, etc.)

🍄 Grab the team and head to the airport to welcome someone returning from a trip.

🍄 Assign "secret jesters" to perform totally anonymous acts of "random fun and humor" on co-workers.

🍄 Create a wacky "start of the workday" and/or "end of the workday" team ritual.

🍄 Create a humorous office calendar, customized with funny photos from your workplace and highlighted dates of significance for your organization.

🍄 Celebrate with flair. To celebrate the inaugural flight of Virgin Atlantic Airways between London and New Delhi, British businessman Richard Branson danced a jig on the tarmac while a crane lifted a garland of cloth flowers onto the airplane's nose.

🍄 Vary your reward and appreciation programs. Variety prevents the rewards from being taken for granted ("Gee, it's Tuesday so the boss must be bringing pizza"). Disney Corporation has close to 180 different staff-recognition programs.

🍄 Create a fan club. There are "Rent-a-Fan" agencies now, where you can hire your own fan club. Even Senegalese President Abdou Diouf is followed everywhere by two or three men dressed in bright colors who yell out compliments and blow whistles or kazoo-like noisemakers at the leader. Why not steal this idea for the workplace, and set up fan clubs for different workers on a rotating basis, for new initiatives or major new projects?

🍄 Hold theme days and celebrate holidays. Auto Glass Plus holds quarterly theme days. Their first, a Hawaiian theme day where employees dressed as islanders and managers served lunch, resulted in a record-breaking sales day. Ben and Jerry's Ice Cream holds a "Corporate Day" where employees dress up as corporate hot shots. Southwest Airlines holds annual Halloween costume parties, Thanksgiving poem contests, "chili-offs" and Christmas newsletter design contests. German stockbrokers regularly dress up during the last day of the Mardi Gras. The Odetics robot company has held a 50s day, a sock hop and even a phone-booth-stuffing event. There is a company that holds a "Dress Like Your Co-worker" day and a Mastercard office in St. Louis that has a "Dress Your Supervisor" day. Anything is possible, and with a little imagination you can tie the theme to one of your products or services. If you're worried about how people might show up (for example, in thong bikinis on Beach Day), then provide a few simple guidelines.

🎤 Police sometimes reward "Good Driving Citations," handing out coupons for free coffee as a combination public relations/educational program. Dole out your own good citation tickets for specific, positive workplace "infractions." (Remember, you get what you reward!)

🎤 Post photos of staff on bulletin boards with changeable humorous cartoon speech or thought bubbles coming out of each person's mouth.

🎤 Give out "I Need-a-Laugh" vouchers that employees can cash in with each other when they are feeling de-motivated or stressed out.

🎤 Establish company teams that include activities anyone can participate in, regardless of physical constraints or level of experience. Many companies have corporate baseball teams, hockey teams or running clubs; so why not a corporate darts club, jazz band, bowling team, book club, chess team, or kite flying, walking, gardening, sky diving or yoga club?

🎤 Hold a mini warm-up meeting 10 minutes each and every morning to rev everyone's engines. Ask everyone how they are doing on a scale from 1 to 10, then offer a reward to the lowest-scoring person to help boost their morale.

🎤 Create some wacky rubber stamps for use on inter-office correspondence like I LOVE THIS IDEA! or WOW!

🎤 Many hospitals have humor carts, so why not create one for your office? Fill it with fun books, wacky prizes and toys and once a month assign someone to roam the halls with it.

🎤 Keep a journal or log book in a highly visible location where people can list their successes.

🎤 Hold a family open house for family members to get to see where employees work.

🎤 Hold regular employee reunions, and invite retirees and former employees to regular staff celebrations like Christmas parties or summer barbecues. The Amy's Ice Cream chain in Austin, Texas, has a "Scooper Reunion" as part of its major anniversary celebrations.

🎤 E-mail out a new "Meet _____" photo each week with a different employee's picture and a humorous bio or funny caption. Larry Halverson, a communications manager in Parks Canada, routinely forwards wacky photos via e-mail as a fun way for people in his vast territory to get to know each other.

🦟 Be silly just for the sake of being silly. The City Council in Syracuse, New York recently passed a bylaw prohibiting any more snow. Now that's just silly.

🦟 Include some casual dress days. There's a huge debate about whether companies have gone too far with "casual Fridays," but a study in Hawaii suggested that on casual Fridays, 81% of employees felt morale was higher, while 47% thought productivity was greater.

🦟 Look for simple ways to motivate each other by acting on spontaneous whims. Turn your phone into mouse ears by placing the receiver over your head upside down and leading the crew in a rousing rendition of the Mickey Mouse theme song. Page yourself (in your own voice) on the PA system or page a co-worker by adding Dr. to their name (this doesn't seem to work if they're already a real doctor). Yell out "dance break" and leap onto your desk and start dancing. Hold an impromptu paper airplane-making contest. Just do something to energize your brains, bodies and wake yourself and your colleagues up!

🦟 Don't forget to say thanks to the support team—the families of employees. We all know that work carries over into our personal lives, success is often tied to supportive families back home. So if an employee has worked long hours (and missed dinner at home) or is on the road a lot, send a thank you card, movie tickets or flowers to the family. Black and Decker sends flowers to spouses on their birthdays or when the working spouse has to travel a lot. Ehvert Technology Services holds a "Fun Night" with fun family events every sixth Friday.

🦟 Create a regular humor column as part of your company newsletter, annual report or web site. Include funny stories, work-related jokes and bloopers, fun announcements, book and movie reviews – anything that adds a little fun, warmth and human spirit.

🦟 Post a humorous quote, question or trivia item each day in a prominent place.

☂ Send a humorous e-greeting card. At www.bluemountain.com you'll find an amazing assortment of work-related cyber cards, including cards for dozens of specific professions, get well cards, thank you cards, motivational cards, seasonal holiday cards and even "I Heard Your Computer Got a Bug" condolence cards.

☂ Have an employee do a weekly/monthly home video or slide show during lunch hour.

☂ Devise a company song, slogan or chant. The sillier (as opposed to corny or schmaltzy) you make it, the better the chance that staff will embrace it and have fun with it. Some employees of Southwest Airlines created a rap song about having fun on the job. And Wal-Mart stores are famous for their employee cheers, which vary from store to store. At a Wal-Mart in Calgary, Alberta, employees do the cheer three or four times each day, followed by some stretching exercises. The cheer is as follows:

Give me a W!	W!
Give me an A!	A!
Give me an L!	L!
Give me a squiggly line! (their substitute for the hyphen; they bend their knees, wiggle their hips, then spring upright again)	
Give me an M!	M!
Give me an A!	A!
Give me an R!	R!
Give me a T!	T!
What's that spell!	Wal-Mart!
Who's number one?	The customers!
Cha-ching!	Cha-ching! (the sound of a cash register opening)

Although a cheer like this may not be appropriate for your office, and may even seem downright silly, most Wal-Mart employees I spoke with said they loved it. It fosters a sense of camaraderie and playfulness in the workplace, and provides a welcome break to the day.

☂ Add some fun to memos. Include funny quotes, cartoons, scanned photos or, as a few managers I have met are inclined to do, write memos in rhyme for a fun and creative touch. Or write memos on the back of torn off cartoon-a-day desk calendars.

Even Thomas Edison interspersed jokes in his experiment note-books to lighten the load for staff reading through them.

☂ Deliver memos in a fun way. Hire a singing telegram person to deliver them once a year or attach them to a pizza, Frisbee or some other toy.

☂ Turn even the dullest or most routine aspects of work into a game. People who devise mental games while on assembly lines, or customer service reps who make it a game to remember everyone's name or eye color, report being happier and more motivated on the job.

☂ Create a Humor Squad or a Corporate Jesters Team, a group of highly motivated, enthusiastic folks who will help facilitate on-going celebrations, rewards and fun activities. Ben and Jerry's Ice Cream has a "Joy Committee" responsible for injecting fun into the workplace and reviewing "Joy Grant" proposals from employees. Rotate membership on the committee around the office.

☂ Organize your own customized Olympics that tie into your particular profession. Domino's Pizza has an annual Olympics that includes veggie slicing and dough-making events. If you're in the financial or administrative business, then have a dueling-calculators contest, a collate-the-paperwork speed test, or a staple-pulling contest. If you're in the restaurant business, have a serving-obstacle-course contest, order-taking memory challenge or a pancake flip-off. It doesn't matter what you do, with a little creative thought you can come up with contests for any profession.

☂ Create fun rituals or traditions. At the company Play, they have a ritual every Friday at 5:00 p.m. where everyone toasts to all the great things that happened in the past week. At Metrographics, the annual Christmas party wouldn't feel complete without the manager's "Epic Poem" recital.

☂ If you don't have one already, create a fun company mascot.

☂ Assign fun nicknames using people's internal phone numbers to spell out their name. For example, if your last four digits are 3,7,6,4, your nickname could be "FROG."

☂ Keep a Polaroid camera on hand to capture spontaneous moments on film, or have a photo scavenger hunt.

☂ Add fun to those boring, dusty organizational charts by including cartoon icons, employee photos, baby photos or mini-bios along each organizational box.

🌂 Hold fun contests. Metrographics in Calgary held a paper airplane contest, where employees, using standardized sheets of paper, launched their crafts off the fourth-story fire escape of a building across from their office. The winner was rewarded with $100.

🌂 Create a fun physical work environment. In chapter 3, we discussed how a fun atmosphere can do wonders for our frame of mind, stress levels, creativity and motivation. So put up humorous photos, signs or posters, set up a humor bulletin board, display your company mascot or create a humor room.

🌂 Hold a spur-of-the-moment contest. On the set of a recent film, Bruce Willis brought in 50 donuts for the crew and cast. When someone joked about how many donuts they could eat, Willis organized a donut-eating contest, offering $100 to whoever could down the most donuts in the shortest time.

> *When you inject a level of playfulness, employees find a common ground. They're reminded they're all on the same side.*
> — Carl Robinson

Wartime Humor

During the London blitz in World War II, humor is thought to have played a large role in bolstering the morale of troops and civilians alike. If it helped an entire nation during a world war, surely humor can help Monday mornings go a little more smoothly at your workplace.

KEEP IT PUMPING!

After returning to work after quadruple bypass surgery, talk show host David Letterman was greeted with a giant banner in the office windows opposite his office with a heartwarming message for the quirky host: "KEEP IT PUMPING DAVE!"

Who's Your Designated Clown?

In 1945, folklorist L.H. Charles discovered 56 different cultures worldwide that had some sort of institutionalized comic role or ceremony as an integral part of their culture. For example, the Zuni (an American aboriginal tribe) had Koyemci clowns, who were significant members of the tribe and members of the priestly class. Both the priest and the clown were well respected by Zuni tribe members, and influenced important matters in society. The clowns influenced society by mocking taboo subject matters that otherwise may not have been discussed. So why not take a page from their book, and assign your own corporate clown or jester?

> *One can discover more about a person in an hour of play than in a year of conversation.*
> — Plato

> *Humor and laughter in organizations can increase the amount of feedback you get, the honesty and the capacity for people to do good things. It's through humor you open up the lines of communication.*
> — Ken Blanchard

Phone Home

On December 4, 1999, when NASA lost the signal to the Mars Polar Lander (MPL), the members of the MPL science team were understandably distraught. To keep their spirits up, each scientist held up a one-letter sign to the media, spelling out the message: "MPL PHONE HOME."

Good Morning!

Larry Halverson, naturalist and CEO (Chief Energizing Officer) for Kootenay National Park, shows how easily workplace rituals can add a little humor seasoning to the start of your day. Larry and a fellow manager, Perry Jacobson, turned their "Good Morning" greetings into a game (it just sort of morphed into one over time as these things are apt to do). The object was simply to beat the other fella' to the punch by wishing him a "Morning Lar'" or a "Morning Per'" first. Before long, they began lurking behind doorways, springing out of cupboards and crouching under the coffee room table in order to be the first with their morning salutation. Larry eventually relied on a little strategic insider help. When Perry awoke one workday morning, his wife tapped him on the shoulder and greeted him with, "Larry says 'Morning Perry!'"

Fun at the Speed of Light!

When Albert A. Michelson, a Nobel Peace Prize winner for science, was asked why he spent so much of his life measuring the velocity of light, he replied, "Because it was fun!"

He deserves paradise who makes his companions laugh.
— The Koran

FINDING WORKPLACE HUMOR IN THE UNLIKELIEST OF PLACES

Now that you have several dozen fun ideas to mull over, let's have a look at a few examples of humor and fun in places you'd never expect.

Even Funeral Directors Need to Laugh

If you think you've got it tough keeping your enthusiasm up, just imagine remaining motivated in the funeral business. At a recent National Funeral Directors Association convention, the topic of "lightening up" surfaced, as directors realized the need not only to maintain their morale, but also to change their image. More and more funeral services now offer creative and highly customized ceremonies aimed at revolutionizing the business. Coroners, another profession that confronts the grim reality of death on a daily basis, must also work hard to maintain their sanity and morale. In an article in *Monday Magazine* by T.K. Demmings, Coroner Lisa Lapointe suggested that sometimes the only way to deal with the horror of her job is to laugh. "We are never laughing at the deceased or the relatives, but at ourselves and our reactions. You have to normalize it."

So Sue Me, I'm Having Fun!

We've all heard dozens of lawyer jokes. But joking around at the law firm of Schiff, Hardin and Waite is no joke. The members of this Chicago-based law firm take their fun seriously, and to prove it they have their very own "Manager of Mischief" (yes, that's her real job title) in the form of one Marceline O'Connor Johnson. Formerly the Manager of Marketing and Communications for the 240-plus law firm, this Manager of Mischief works in the Fun Department, alongside the firm's Director of Fun and Creator of Celebrations. According to Johnson, her role came about partly because they wanted to "position marketing, something that is uncomfortable for most attorneys, as pleasurable." In their Fun Department lawyers can de-stress with the usual assortment of stress-reducing toys including magic wands, slinkys, stress balls, castanets and goofy sculptures. The Fun Department also doles out goodies like chocolates, canvas bags and flashlights to lawyers who have a marketing idea or who have worked on a marketing project. They've even sent memos out in rhyme and gotten them back in rap verse from managing partners. And to help keep spirits high, they've coordinated ice cream socials for staff (with the executive committee doing the serving) and have included magicians, caricaturists and even tarot card readers at company dinners. Besides helping lawyers relax and have fun, part of her role is to help their clients see lawyers as real human beings. According to Johnson, clients have e-mailed the firm and complimented them on their more "human approach" to practicing law.

We Want You ... To Have Fun!

Surely to goodness we'll never find fun in the American armed forces, will we? We're beginning to. In 1991, during the Gulf War, the Pentagon sent 20,000 Frisbees to troops to boost their morale. And the *Benfold USS*, an American aircraft carrier, is known for its high morale and motivated troops. They've held Elvis impersonation contests, pumpkin-carving contests and played music videos on the side of the ship.

Is There Something in the Fish?

At world famous Pike's Fish Market in Seattle, Washington, there's something fishy going on. Local area office workers make a point to swing by this fun-filled, high energy, zany fish market on their lunch hour just to watch the workers having fun. This small market has made a name for itself by creating a mini-cyclone of fun and energy in everything they do. On a typical day, workers at the fish market enthusiastically toss fish back and forth, sing crazy songs, dance and energetically interact with customers.

People have asked me in a rather cynical tone, "How can those fish guys really love their jobs that much? Surely, it's not the greatest job in the world?" And they're absolutely right. Schlepping fish isn't likely high on anyone's list of dream jobs. The employees at Pike's Fish Market, however, offer the perfect example of how people really do choose the attitude they bring to work everyday. Most of us don't live the glamorous life of royalty, fly the Space Shuttle or get paid $20 million per movie. Which leaves only one option: choose your attitude—even when you're staring at fish heads all day.

> *It's important to have a collegial, supportive, yeasty, zany, laughter-filled environment where folks support each other.*
>
> — Tom Peters

WANTED: CORPORATE JESTER TO LIVEN UP OFFICE

The practice of workplace humor has been around a long time. Industrial sociologists have observed that "on the job joking and bantering" as a means of building unity, relieving tension and reducing the tedium of boring manual labor has been a ritualized part of the workforce since the Industrial Revolution. Going back even farther, jesters first emerged around the time of the early Egyptian pharaohs. And later, the Court Jester (not to be confused with the "court gesture," which is often obscene and not terribly appropriate) provided an excellent role model for modern-day corporate humor.

Court jesters arrived on the scene around 1000 AD. William the Conqueror (no, not Bill Gates) may have had one of the first jesters, a jocular fellow named Goles, who evidently helped William lighten up after a hard day of conquering. Court jesters were respected members of the royal inner circle; in fact, many leaders used their jester as a confidante and took advice from him. By using humor, jesters could point out sensitive truths to a leader that other members of the court could not. They were especially relied on during times of war, as a means of relieving stress. King Henry III used his jester to overcome sadness, while Queen Elizabeth I reported that her jester cured her melancholy better than any doctor could. Alas, jesters petered out during the 1600s, after the government tried to license them (leave it to the bureaucrats to break up a good laugh-fest).

So why not take a lesson from the past and hire or create your own *corporate* jester—someone with wit, wisdom, storytelling abilities and a snappy sense of fashion. Your jester could become a cheerleader for the company and a morale booster when times are tough, and hand out surprise rewards, interrupt shareholder meetings with a great joke or juggle during wearisome sales presentations.

At the *very* least, we should revive the *spirit* of the Court Jester (minus the part where they get beheaded for not being funny).

> *The jester is a brother of the scientist and the artist.*
> — Arthur Koestler

FINAL THOUGHT -
ARE YOU SPENDING TOO MUCH TIME
CONQUERING?

Diogenes the Cynic, an ancient Greek philosopher, once grilled Alexander the Great about his career plans. Alexander said he wished to conquer Greece. "And then?" pondered Diogenes. "Conquer Asia Minor." "And then what?" continued Diogenes. "Conquer and subjugate the entire world," replied Alexander.

"And then what?" asked Diogenes one last time. Alexander responded by saying he would then relax and enjoy himself, to which Diogenes (being the clever philosopher he was) replied, "Why not save yourself a lot of time and trouble by relaxing and enjoying yourself now?"

And that seems to be the ideal quote to end this chapter on. Although "Alexander the Relaxer" may not have made it into the history books, what's *your* excuse for not enjoying your work more often, starting right now?

"You should see him when the paper clips arrive."

— 8 —

Laughing Your Way to Better Customer Service

We've all heard the phrase "service with a smile." Why not carry this slogan one step further and offer customer service with some laughter? After all, if practicing humor inside your organization can achieve all kinds of wonderful advantages, why *wouldn't* you extend those same benefits to the people most important to the success of your business? Including customers in the fun loop can help you find new customers, retain loyal customers and diffuse potential customer complaints. (And I hate to sound like a broken record here, but practicing humor will also improve your coffee, and really, what customer wouldn't appreciate that?)

WE NEED CUSTOMERS!

In this increasingly competitive, international, dog-eat-dingo, internet-savvy marketplace, finding customers is a challenge. Keeping them is even harder. Customers are more knowledgeable and demanding than ever before. And one of the things customers demand is quality service that shows a company and you, the person working for the company, care about them beyond their pocketbook. Advertising and promotional materials that convey a humorous touch not only grab people's attention, but can also send the message, loud and humorously, that you care about your customers as people first.

Consumers are bombarded with close to 1,500 ads on a typical day. Humor is one of the most effective means of getting attention in this overcrowded marketplace and standing out from the herd. It's no wonder close to three-quarters of all television and radio ads rely on humor to grab the audience by the funny bone. If you recall some of your favorite ads, 9 times out of 10, you'll find they made you laugh. In fact, close to 70% of the ads that win awards contain humor. So obviously at the mass-market level of advertising, those media-wise ad folks realize the potent power of humor. But what about using some attention-grabbing humor techniques on a smaller scale? If it works for television and radio ads, then add a humorous touch to your yellow page ads, newspaper ads, signs and even your business cards. *Any* point of contact with potential customers offers the opportunity to tap them on their funny bone.

A Bug Only a Mother Could Love

The Volkswagen company is credited as being a pioneer in the use of self-effacing humor in advertising. Until humorous VW commercials arrived in the 1960s, advertisers shied away from using humor to sell products. But with VW ads such as "a face only a mother could love" that laughed at themselves, attitudes began to shift. Humor quickly became a staple ingredient in advertising campaigns.

Hey Potato Head! Get Your Customers' Attention!

A humorous mascot is an easy way to grab your customers' attention. The state of Rhode Island knows this. They've adopted "Mr. Potato Head" as their mascot as part of their "Rhode Island - Birthplace of Fun" campaign, in an effort to market their state as a fun and family-friendly tourism destination. Dozens of six-foot-high statue versions of famed childhood toy "Mr. Potato Head" throughout the state remind people that Rhode Island is a fun place to visit. (I tried to get a quote about how the campaign is going, but unfortunately, Mr. Potato Head was unavailable for comment.)

OPTION #1   OPTION #2

Who would *you* rather do business with?

GUIDING LIGHTS FOR USING HUMOR
WITH YOUR CUSTOMERS

It's worth reinforcing some basic humor principles before we think about extending our laugh lines to include our customers.

1. Practice ultra safe humor. Practicing safe humor is critical when you expand your audience to include your customers. Your customers come from all walks of life and backgrounds, so tread very carefully—keep all humor clean and positive.

When it comes to advertising, unsafe humor can be costly. After a public outcry, Absolut Vodka pulled ads that poked fun at ski mishaps, BC Tel was forced to remove ads that were deemed insulting to prairie folks, while Ford of Canada had to remove ads that tried to humorously portray used car salesmen as irresponsible business people. (For the complete lowdown on practicing safe humor, see chapter 12.)

2. Practice relevant humor. To reinforce your image and your company's name and services, link the humor, whenever possible, with the products or services you are selling. WestJet Airlines, for example, tells airline-related jokes on their flights.

3. Keep it simple, silly. The old "KISS principle" applies even here. Look for simple, day-to-day opportunities to slip in a little humor.

4. Maintain a professional image. Ultimately, your customers demand service and professionalism at all times, not a stand-up comedian (unless you are a stand-up comedian, in which case, you better be providing the laughs loud and fast).

5. Blend the humor. Look for ways to mix humor into your existing services. Think of humor as *part* of the service, not an add-on after the fact. There are all sorts of missed opportunities out there waiting for an injection of fun.

6. Keep service staff happy. The key to having happy customers is having happy staff. One of Southwest Airlines' beliefs is "the customer is number two!" They believe that by treating employees as the top priority, they, in turn, will treat customers as their top priority. So look for ways to continually add humor, passion and fun to the front line of service delivery.

SERVICE WITH A LAUGH

There are dozens of simple ways to inject a little humor into all areas of your customer service. Here are just a few ideas to start the fun wheels rolling.

Include humor on your business cards. A funny slogan, snappy quote or fun picture will help ensure people not only remember you, but hold onto your business card, and better yet, share it with others. My company business card for Speaking of Ideas includes the following list along the bottom of the card:

Speaker * Trainer *Author * Consultant * Nice Guy

The "Nice Guy" part always catches people's attention—I've even had clients phone me to ask if it's true (yes, yes it is).

One of my favorite business cards belongs to Dr. Joel Goodman, director of The Humor Project in Saratoga Springs, New York. On the back of his business card is a list of "Important Phone Numbers," including fake telephone numbers for the President, the Pope, and Queen Elizabeth, finishing, naturally, with his own phone number.

Fun business cards are the norm at the company Play, in Richmond, Virginia. Although the cards themselves are square (literally), what's on them is anything but. All employees have a card featuring a photo of them striking a playful pose, and including their unique job titles such as the "Flying Buttress."

Another memorable approach to humorizing business cards is to use sound card holders, which, upon opening, make a sound (hence the name, "sound cards," silly). These cards are available in dozens of different sounds, including ones that laugh, giggle, howl or sneeze when opened.

Include humor on signs to catch people's attention or soften authoritative messages. For example:

A sign in a small store in Canmore, Alberta, which sells many fragile items, cautions customers to watch their children with a sign:
This Store is Rated PG: Parental Guidance is Advised.

Sign in a restaurant:
You Are Welcome to Use Our Smoking Room. It is Located Outdoors.

Sign in the parking lot of a veterinarian clinic:
No Parking. Violators Will Be Neutered.

Sign in a radiator shop:
Best Place in Town to Take a Leak.

Sign on a small restaurant:
Eat Here or We'll Both Starve.

Sign on a plumbing store:
A Flush Beats a Full House.

Sign in a small gift shop in Mexico selling used golf balls:
For Sale: Experienced Golf Balls.

Sign seen in many restaurants:
The bank doesn't make sandwiches and we don't cash cheques.

Sign in many other restaurants:
If you think my service is bad, you should see my manager.

Sign in bathroom of a store:
We aim to please, so, please, you aim too.

Sign at the Hole in the Wall Café/Gas Station, in Cadomin, Alberta:
Eat Here & Get Gas.

A sign on an IRS office window in the United States:
Sorry We're In.

A very memorable, attention-getting sign is found on the outside wall of Metrographics, a graphics design company based in Calgary, Alberta. The giant mural featuring Mona Lisa was painted by the general manager Doug Driediger. The Mona Lisa delivers messages to thousands of motorists every day via her continually changing speech bubble. As Driediger explained, "The sign helps act as a spokesperson for us. It speaks to our style. The sign helps us sell our friendly, casual and creative approach to business." The messages include public service announcements, amusing thoughts or wacky ideas about current events affecting Calgary. For example, during a debate about the use of fluoride in the Calgary water system, the Mona sign said, "Skip fluoride . . . let's put caffeine in the water!" During a particularly stressful week at Metrographics, the message in the speech bubble was: "We're having a rough week. Please give chocolate." Driediger was amazed at the response the message generated when people actually dropped by with chocolate treats for the staff!

Develop a humorous slogan. Canmore, Alberta, dentist Dr. Josée C. Bourgon uses the slogan "We cater to cowards" in her ads and newsletters. The slogan of my Corporate Jesters company is "We Won't Take Your Business Seriously."

Add some humor to your voice mail system or answering machine. For example, add a "Press 5 if you are now totally confused" or throw in something incongruous like "Press 7 for weather information from Bora Bora."

The king of automated phone humor has to be WestJet Airlines. While waiting on hold for the next available operator, WestJet offers customers a high energy, informative and humorous commentary that makes you hope the operators will actually take their time before getting to your call. The running commentary includes sound effects, tongue twisters ("try saying frequent flyer points five times") trivia, ("did you know 'stewardess' is the longest word you can type solely with your left hand?"), jokes and goofy advice ("don't run with scissors"), all intermixed with information about routes, carry-on requirements and selling points. They even practice a little self-effacing airline humor by announcing the new $300 service to Fiji, followed promptly with a loud "just kidding!" And at one point they suggest that if you've waited too long, you should press *15, adding quickly that this of course won't help, but you may feel better anyway. Adding this humorous touch helps reduce the perceived waiting time, keeps customers on the line relaxed and in a good mood, helps them soft sell other services and sends the message they are a fun, service-oriented company.

Create a fun waiting room or meeting place. Having fun reading materials, an oversized model of the company mascot, a humor bulletin board, a quote of the day board, fun signs or a company photo album for customers in a reception area is an ideal way to lighten their mood and convey a warm welcome. If you have an intercom and a reception area where several people are typically waiting, then pipe over the occasional joke or humorous update about how long they'll have to wait. Or try doling out a few small door prizes for people waiting a long time. At WestJet terminals, check-in agents sometimes offer small prizes for whoever has the oldest penny or whoever can guess the combined age of the three agents working at the counter.

You could make your office so much fun, that even a trip to the dentist would seem painless. In Orlando, Florida, Dr. Denis Bourguigon's dental office features a *Star Trek* theme. Every inch of the office is covered with *Star Trek* images and gadgets. Even the staff dress up as members of the *Starship Enterprise*. Adult clients love the relaxed and off-beat setting as much as the children do.

Similarly, Dr. Gordon Chin, based in Calgary, Alberta, tries to make a trip to the dentist as painless as possible. According to Dr. Chin, his dental office is designed to create a homey atmosphere. The office includes video games, a Polaroid photo wall of happy child patients, an aquarium, VCRs and even a putting green. As Dr. Chin says, "By focusing on fun, service and the patient's comfort, we make sure that people have a good time so they come back."

Add humor into any regulations or instructions. Just once, while putting together a do-it-yourself kit, I'd love to read the following instruction: "Step 7: Throw down your tools in disgust and kick the wall, while making loud under-your-breathe cursing sounds."

Take advantage of a captive audience. Both WestJet and Southwest Airlines are known for their in-flight humor. Even when the jokes are groaners, passengers seem to appreciate the gesture. Southwest Airlines goes one step further by not only telling wacky jokes, but also frequently reviewing the safety instructions in a lighthearted manner, donning funny costumes or singing songs to convey the otherwise routine messages that frequent fliers have heard hundreds of times.

Take advantage of spontaneous moments. While I was at a major department store, a cashier got on the intercom and let everyone know that it was a fellow employee's birthday. She then led the entire store, customers and all, through a rousing rendition of "Happy Birthday" over the intercom. Similarly, General Mills took advantage of a spontaneous incident when seven-year-old Perley King of Tacoma, Washington, drove off in his sister's car in search of a box of Cheerios. General Mills representatives visited Perley and presented him with a bike and a year's supply of Cheerios so he'd never

How to Quack Up Your Customers

National Discount Brokers, an online brokerage firm, discovered that small gestures can reap huge rewards after adding a humorous touch to their toll free voice mail system. When customers phone their 1-800 number they now have the option of pressing 7 if they want to hear a duck quack (their company mascot is a mallard). Once news of the "toll free quack" circulated on the internet, phone calls went through the roof. The company averaged two million phone calls a week and increased their new accounts by 75 percent.

have to drive to the store again. Airline pilots often take advantage of spontaneous moments to interject some humor over the intercom during a flight or after a landing. One pilot, on a recent flight I was on, welcomed everyone to Calgary after a particularly rough landing with, "Your stomach should be arriving momentarily." And taking advantage of a truly earth-shattering event, many Seattle bars featured "shaken not stirred" martinis after the 2001 earthquake shook up the local area.

Include customers in theme days or holiday events. If you're having a Hawaiian day, hand out leis and serve punch to the customers. WestJet Airlines offered free flights one year on Valentine's Day to anyone with the last names of Heart(s), Hart(s) or Love(s), while for Thanksgiving they offered the same deal to folks named Bean(s), Barley or Oat(s).

Celebrate internal milestones with the customer. During the summer of 1999, Volkswagen celebrated their 50th anniversary of the first Beetle imported into the United States with a day-long party known as "DriverFest," an event that will likely carry on as an annual celebration.

Say thanks to your customers in a creative way. At Amy's Ice Cream stores in Austin, Texas, customers still in the store after closing hour sometimes get an impromptu lesson on how to dance the "time warp." I send clients humorous small gifts, like clown noses, as a way to say thanks and remind them of my message and services.

Send thank you cards to your clients on unexpected occasions. Groundhog Day, Halloween or April Fool's Day are great choices. (I'm sending out Happy Humor Month cards for April to my clients. If you haven't received one yet, either you're not one of my clients or it's in the mail.)

Look for fun ways to get more exposure. The IRS in the United States sold Christmas ornaments with "Many Happy Returns" on them. Marra's Grocery store in Canmore, Alberta, encourages customers to submit photos of them traveling afar with a picture of their Marra's grocery bag. The "traveling bag" photos get displayed on a store wall and featured in the local newspaper. Taco Bell offered everyone in the United States a free taco if the core of the decommissioned Mir space station hit a giant floating target off Australia.

Dole out fun prizes and rewards for customers. Have a fun reward for the 100th customer of the day or week. Give out a prize for the most loyal customer of the year, or the client with the most outlandish tie collection or dish out small treats for anyone celebrating a birthday. The possibilities are truly limitless. There is a bus driver in Hawaii known for handing out leis to passengers who need cheering up. The minor-league baseball team Charleston RiverDogs, who have held events like "Bill Murray Mask Night," had a controversial giveaway draw tied to Father's Day – a free vasectomy.

Hold fun contests. The Alberta-based telecommunications company Fido held a dog and owner look-alike contest to generate some positive PR. As many companies have done, you could hold a contest to involve customers in devising a new company slogan, mascot or advertising campaign.

Add a humorous quote or cartoon to your invoices or receipts. Whenever I forward an invoice for services rendered, I always include a "Smile-on-a-Stick®" in hopes that I'll cheer up someone's day and, more to the point, get my money faster.

Use humor to improve your own customer service skills. A New York bank improved customer service by displaying posters that humorously

Customer Service With a Smile

Here are a few nearing-the-end-of-the-chapter points to help bring a smile to your face when thinking about the importance of "service with a smile."

"A smile is the shortest distance between two people." Victor Borge

Our smile is the facial expression most visible from the farthest distance; we can see that a person is smiling as far as 100 feet (30 meters) away.

Smiles may have evolved as a means of communicating: "I mean no harm, I will not bite, and to prove it I am showing you my teeth."

Psychologists say it's easier to remember happy memories when we smile.

There are 18 different types of smiles.

Smiling can reduce stress by cooling the blood temperature going to the hypothalamus.

A fake smile can produce the same physical benefits as a genuine smile.

"If you're not using your smile, you're like a man with a million dollars in the bank, and no check book." Les Giblin

People can tell when the person on the other end of a phone call is smiling or not by the change in the tone of voice.

Women tend to smile more than men, especially for photographs.

"Wrinkles should merely indicate where the smiles have been." Mark Twain

Waitresses who smile more receive, on average, 18% higher tips.

It takes 50 muscles to frown but only 13 muscles to smile.

"A smile is a curve that sets everything straight." Phyllis Diller

When Mom told us that if we "kept making that silly face it might stay that way permanently," she was partially right. The facial lines and contours we carry into old age are largely a direct result of the prominent facial expressions we walk around with throughout our lives. So start smiling now!

poked fun at some of the common mistakes tellers make. Humorous slogans, buttons, posters, top-10 lists and signs can help remind front line staff of the importance of delivering dynamic customer service. Another fun way to foster better customer service in certain businesses is to have your own staff members be a "customer for a day," where they go through the entire customer experience from start to finish.

Use humor to help service employees relieve their stress. Dealing with irate or difficult customers is a huge source of stress for many workers, and interestingly, some researchers have found that the old maxim "the customer is always right" often causes employees to feel more stressed. When staff are forced into a "grin and bear it with gritted teeth" mode, they often end up holding their emotions inside like a bottled-up genie. Taking a humor break, reframing a bad situation humorously or offering a reward for whoever best handles the "Customer from Hell" can relieve stress and help promote fantastic customer service in the face of trying clients.

CLOSING THOUGHTS

Everyone pays lip service to customer service. But very few organizations back it up with memorable service that truly wows their clients each and every time. And yet small gestures can make an enormous impression. So whether your clients are internal or external, virtual or in the flesh, take the time to think about a few ways you can add a touch of humor to their customer experience. Service with some laughter is service that won't be easily forgotten.

— 9 —

We've <u>GOT</u> to Stop Meeting Like This!

The real origin of the term "boardroom."

If you haven't been to a meeting lately, chances are you are: A) dead, B) trapped under something heavy, C) taking a phone message for someone who *is* at a meeting, D) all of the above. Everyone's meeting. And if you're not meeting someone right now, you're obviously not getting any work done. There are breakfast, lunch and dinner meetings (but curiously, no midnight-snack meetings), power meetings, information meetings and brainstorming meetings. There are emergency meetings and regular "because-it's-Tuesday-morning" meetings. There are corporate retreats (why are we retreating when we should be advancing?), virtual meetings and in-the-flesh meetings (not to be mistaken for nudist camp meetings where everyone really is in the flesh). There are four-hour meetings to talk about how unproductive meetings are. And there are even pre-meetings to discuss upcoming meetings and post-meetings to review how past meetings went.

And don't for a meeting minute think that it's just corporate types who are meeting. Obviously you've forgotten about the neighborhood clean-up meeting, the City Council meeting, the Boy Scouts meeting, all followed closely by the condominium association meeting. Like death and taxes, you can hide for a while, but you can never truly escape meetings. (I'm pretty sure there are meetings in the afterlife, so even death isn't really an option if you're looking for the definitive way to avoid them.)

How much time do we spend in meetings? Too much, is the obvious answer. According to one source, average North Americans will spend three years of their life in business meetings, while Chic Thompson, author of *What a Great Idea!*, suggests that more than 11 million meetings take place in the United States each day, and close to 70 million meetings worldwide. One stressed-out executive confessed she was *so* busy attending meetings she didn't have time to attend *other* meetings. We know we're in trouble, folks, when our meetings start cutting into our meetings.

Business people tell me they spend anywhere from 30 to 80% of their week in meetings. Many have suggested that attending meetings is *all they do* at work, to the point where some of them think of themselves as "professional meeters." By one frightening count, many people spend more time in meetings than they spend making love, getting physical exercise or enjoying quality time with their dog. Clearly, a lot of time, energy and whiteboard markers are being sucked up by meetings. (Here's an idea: maybe we could just have one *big* meeting with everyone right now and save ourselves a lot of time down the road)

So what's the result of all these meetings? Meeting phobia, meetingitis and meeting anxiety disorder (M.A.D.) are just a few of the workplace ailments inflicting us. Numerous workplace surveys suggest that meetings are one of the most dreaded aspects of many workers' jobs, contributing to low morale, frustration and stress. Clearly, we've *got* to stop meeting like this!

The Top-10 Signs
You Are Meeting WAY Too Often

10. You prepare a formal agenda each time you make love to your spouse.

9. You feel the need to second your child's motion for more apple pie.

8. You insist all family members wear a "Hi, My name is . . ." sticky badge to dinner.

7. You hold brainstorming sessions with your dog.

6. You have a whiteboard in your shower.

5. You assign a secretary to record minutes from the breakfast table.

4. Your favorite part of a STAR TREK episode is when the captain calls everyone together for an emergency meeting.

3. You've converted your den into a spare boardroom, "just in case."

2. You have your own monogrammed laser pointer.

1. You secretly crash other organizations' meetings on your day off.

DILBERT reprinted by permission of United Feature Syndicate, Inc.

WHY WE HATE MEETINGS –
LET US COUNT THE WAYS

It's not just the amount of time we spend in meetings, it's the lack of *quality* time we're spending together that frustrates most of us. Here are some of the main beefs people express about meetings.

1. They are too long.*

2. There are too many.

3. They never accomplish anything.

4. They lack any coherent purpose.

5. "I don't need to be there half the time."

6. They are too tense.

7. They create meaningless work.

8. There are too many hidden agendas around the table and no one ever speaks the truth.

9. All talk, no action (see #3 & 7).

10. They are not run properly (see #1-14).

11. We just talk in circles (see # 3, 7 & 9).

12. The coffee is horrible.

13. No one ever brings donuts.

14. They are no fun!

*According to one survey, the average person (that could be you) believes that over 50% of the time spent in meetings is wasted. Employees of large organizations are also more likely to complain about meetings than workers in smaller companies, adding further credence to the old saying that good things sometimes come in small packages.

Clearly we have some issues that need addressing (perhaps we should convene a meeting to discuss them?). Although the rest of this chapter focuses on the "meetings aren't fun" problem, because humor helps in so many ways, you'll likely also improve some of the other issues along the way.

A Brief History of Meetings

The earliest recorded meeting occurred when Adam met Eve, and we all know how that went. The first true brainstorming meeting occurred when a group of cave people met in Thog's cave to come up with a better idea than a square wheel. Since they didn't have whiteboards they had to draw their ideas on cave walls, making meetings even longer than they are today. So the long and the short of it is this: we've been meeting since the dawn of time—and probably before that, because someone had to decide when the dawn of time was actually going to begin.

I think they should consider giving Oscars for meetings: Best Meeting of the Year, Best Supporting Meeting, Best Meeting Based on Material from Another Meeting.
— William Goldman

WHY WE SHOULD ADD SOME FUN TO OUR MEETINGS – LET US COUNT THE REASONS

Recall one of the basic myths we slew in chapter 1: just because we're meeting about something that's important or we work in a "serious profession conducting serious business," doesn't mean we have to take *ourselves* seriously. This is especially true when ourselves are hunkered around a table staring at an agenda in a room aptly called the *bored*room with someone at the head of the table with the ominous title of chairperson. The formality that has oozed its way into many of our meetings is designed to help keep us organized, on track and efficient. So efficient, that most of us can easily list at least 14 reasons why everyone hates meetings (sorry, this is an example of sarcasm, something I promised myself I'd keep to a minimum).

Some people worry that nothing will get accomplished if we make meetings fun. But I am not suggesting meeting anarchy and chaos. Meetings still need a well-defined purpose, planned agenda and a skilled facilitator to keep people focused and moving along. The humor input should be viewed as a complementary catalyst that, rather than detracting from the meeting at hand, results in a more efficient and productive meeting. Onward then, with a few reasons why you just *can't* be serious during meetings.

Adding Humor to Meetings Can . . .

1. Get people to show up (and on time).

2. Make people actually want to be there.

3. Spark ideas during creativity meetings.

4. Encourage open dialogue.

5. Build trust between people.

6. Foster a sense of teamwork.

7. Promote positive behavior.

8. Discourage unwanted behavior in a non-threatening way.

9. Make business presentations more effective and memorable (or how about just bearable!).

10. Help meeting attendees retain the meeting information. (If folks can't remember the meeting, how are they supposed to remember what was said?)

11. Reduce escalating conflicts and keep communication flowing on a positive channel.

12. Reduce stress levels.

13. Keep people awake (always a good minimum goal).

14. Leave participants feeling energized and excited after a meeting (versus beaten up, spent and demoralized).

Now please go back and compare the 14 common complaints about meetings with this list of 14 benefits of adding humor. If you are still unsure about the need to add humor to your next meeting, place your index finger firmly on your wrist and check for a pulse. (I know this sounds a little harsh, but *really!*)

> *We rarely succeed at anything unless we are having fun doing it.*
> — Reverend John Naus

The Four Features of a Successful Meeting

According to research reported in Tropman's MAKING MEETINGS WORK: ACHIEVING HIGH QUALITY GROUP DECISIONS (1996), an effective meeting contains these elements:

- Decisions are made; there is a sense of accomplishment.

- Decisions are not re-decided; participants don't waste time reworking previously made decisions.

- The decisions made at meetings are good ones.

- The meeting is fun! People enjoy themselves and have a good time!

THE COMPLETE GUIDE TO ADDING HUMOR TO YOUR MEETINGS

(For the low down on creative brainstorming meetings please see chapter 6.)

1. Create a Fun Agenda

Adding a little humor to the agenda may get people reading the agenda before a meeting and, better yet, attending the meeting. Here are a few ideas.

- Use a fun font type (at *least* in the agenda heading) as a grabber.

- Have a fun title.

- Add cartoons, clip art or scan a humorous photo to the agenda.

- Include a humorous quote or saying alongside each agenda item.

- Put something totally out of place in the middle of the agenda to catch people by surprise (e.g., Item 3: Solve World Peace; or Item 7: The Tomato: Fruit or Vegetable?).

- Intentionally include three mistakes in the agenda and reward people for finding them as a way to encourage people to read the agenda beforehand.

🌴 Incorporate fun subtitles for each item on the agenda. Try developing a theme and name all your agenda points after movie titles, soap operas, famous quotations or songs.

🌴 Put the time allotted beside each agenda item, but exaggerate the times (Decision on My Budgeting Proposal: 5 seconds; Budget Allotment Discussion: 17 hours), or be ridiculously specific (Review Past Meeting Agenda: 10:47:36 a.m. – 10:51:55 a.m.).

🌴 Glue a Hershey Kiss, sucker or some other treat to each agenda.

🌴 Include a "Surprise Mystery" agenda item (and then come up with something fun!).

🌴 Include a redeemable cut-out coupon good for one free donut at the meeting.

2. Make Fun Part of the Agenda

Depending on the meeting length, schedule fun right into the meeting. Even some Native Indian tribes began their spiritual ceremonies with a good laugh. Opening a meeting with some fun sets a positive tone and a humor break in the middle provides much-needed relief, while ending with some fun can leave people feeling upbeat and positive.

More and more companies of all types are making an effort to purposefully blend some humor or even downright zany antics into their regular staff meetings. During meetings at the creative agency Play, there is often time set aside for storytelling, reading from humorous books and even grammar lessons from a staff member dressed as an English teacher. At Showtime Networks Inc., meetings involve lots of jokes, theater, storytelling, music and skits. So build some fun into your next meeting by including one of these ideas.

🌴 Use a fun icebreaker before a brainstorming meeting. (One study found that participants who watched funny videos before brainstorming were 300 to 500% more likely to come up with creative solutions to problems they encountered.)

🌴 Have a fun "get-to-know-each-other" icebreaker before a meeting where people don't know each other.

🌴 Include a 15-minute laugh break in the middle with a fun networking activity.

🍄 Start meetings out on the right foot by creating a tradition of having everyone talk about their most recent success or providing one reason to celebrate.

🍄 Schedule in a fun *Jeopardy!* or *Who Wants to Be a Millionaire* style quiz to give employees a chance to ask the president, CEO or Biggest Cheese in the Room questions about the company.

🍄 Schedule in a "humor mill" section featuring the blooper of the week, funniest incident of the month or the best work-related joke.

🍄 Schedule in a "rumor mill section," a great way to open up communication channels in a non-threatening, humorous manner.

🍄 Schedule in a "whine and cheese" portion to allow participants to share concerns in a fun, exaggerated manner. (Scheduling it for a specific time frame also helps to prevent participants from whining and sniveling throughout the entire meeting.)

🍄 Have a "pick your nose" portion of the meeting where everyone gets to choose their own nose to wear for the duration of the meeting. (Your neighborhood joke store can supply you with everything from pig to walrus noses.)

3. Meet in a Fun Place

Any change in routine, such as meeting at a different time or place, can lead to new perspectives and therefore new ideas. Meeting in a new, neutral location also helps participants feel more relaxed, so meet at the city park, back lawn, bowling alley, museum or at someone's house over breakfast. The change in group dynamics, reduced stress levels and changed perspective can do wonders for a tired meeting routine and allow staff to access their sense of humor more readily. Some alternative meeting locales to ponder include:

City park	Amusement park	Mini golf course	Science center
Bowling alley	Someone's house*	Wilderness lodge	Beach
Arcade	Picnic site	Zoo	Downtown square
Museum	Airport	Hiking trail	Restaurant
Art gallery	Train station	Planetarium	Branch office

*Preferably someone who is actually participating in the meeting

4. Name Your Regular Meeting Room Something Inspired

Who wants to meet in a *bored*room? To inspire means to "breathe life into," so breathe some life into your boardroom by giving it an inspirational name. In one Apple Computer office, the meeting rooms are named after characters in the *Wizard of Oz*. Another company nicknamed their meeting space "The Bridge" in honor of *Star Trek*. MLC corporation has creative meeting spaces that include The Table (with fridges, stoves and a huge wooden table, so people can eat and meet at the same time), the Zen Den (with bamboo sculptures, river stones and Japanese pavilions) and the Forum (a round theater with Spanish steps to encourage lounging and listening). At the Play company, they have a Hall of Justice and, naturally, a Playroom. Johnson and Johnson has the Idea Farm. Yahoo! have meeting rooms named after Ben and Jerry's ice cream flavours. The ultimate room name award, however, goes to the Creative Solutions Network for their meeting space called the THINKubator™.

Here are a few of my own suggestions for an inspiring-sounding boardroom:

The Not-So Boardroom	Creativity Corner	The WOW Room
Idea Central	The Idea Laboratory	The E.R.
Inspiration Point*	The People Place	The Palace

That-Fun-Place-We-All-Meet-And-Have-Fun-Together-Talking-About-Work-Stuff

* Okay, perhaps this sounds too much like a make-out place where teenagers go after the drive-in?

5. Create a Fun Meeting Room Environment

The next best thing to moving your meeting to a fresh location is to design a bright, creative meeting space. Aim for lots of natural light, fun posters, toys and props to inspire creativity and loosen folks up. Odetics, a robot manufacturing company, has a replica of the space shuttle made out of beer cans sitting in its conference meeting room. Employees of the Liberty Toy Company play with foam darts before sitting down to a meeting. You can even use fun music or sound effects to announce the start of a meeting (as the company Play does with their drumming), introduce new agenda items or get people back to their seats after a break. During some meetings at Apple Computer, employees signal their approval using kazoos.

Another simple idea is to hold a few chair-less meetings. Removing the chairs can create a more casual atmosphere conducive to open dialogue. (And by preventing people from getting too comfy, it also helps foster shorter meetings.)

For meetings where people may not know their way to the room, include some fun welcome/directional signs. Post traffic signs along the route, including a cartoon with each directional sign, or post a sign that says "Meeting Room This Way, Escape Route That Way."

Accessories for the Complete Meeting Space

Play Doh	Puzzles	Foam balls	Paper airplanes
Yo-Yos	Funny hats	Slinkies	Foam basketball & hoop
Miniature puzzles	Postcards	Funny noses	Foam darts
Drink parasols	Magnetic poetry	Magic props	Stress balls
Kaleidoscopes	Silly Putty	Lego	Humor books/magazines
Polaroid camera	Goofy staff photos	Staff baby pictures	De-stressor squeeze balls
Noisemakers			

The THINKubator™

Quite possibly the ultimate creative meeting space is found in Chicago, Illinois, at the headquarters of the Creative Solutions Network. Here you'll find the "THINKubator™", the ultimate brainstorming environment, featuring wacky toys, gadgets, customized furniture, a scent sampler, a 500–CD jukebox, a Wall of Wonder and a brainstorm meeting area that converts into a disco. Curtis Sittenfeld, reporting in FAST COMPANY magazine, describes the THINKubator™ as a "combination rec room and art gallery."

6. Introduce Participants in a Fun Way

Not introducing meeting participants is a major breach of social etiquette (and common sense), yet how many of us have attended meetings where people are not introduced properly, if at all? It's a recipe for participants to feel alienated, tense and unwelcome. How people are greeted, welcomed and introduced sets the tone for the entire meeting. So take the time to introduce people and do it with a little flair so they don't feel stressed about the whole process. Here are a few ideas.

🍄 Use name tags, but in addition to their name, ask people to write down something on their tag as an icebreaker, like three numbers that have some significance to them, their childhood hometown or their nickname. These tags can be used later to divide large groups into smaller working groups.

🍄 Create name tags using Polaroid cameras to shoot fun picture-tags on the spot.

🍄 Start the fun as soon as the first person arrives. Don't punish people who arrive early or on time—make sure there is something for them to do or discuss. Have a pre-meeting icebreaker like a puzzle, brainteaser or quiz. Make the icebreaker related to the meeting so it is not only fun, but "value-added" as well. For large meetings with new participants, use a "Human Resources Treasure Hunt/Scavenger Hunt" as a way to get people mingling (see sidebar) .

🍄 Assign a "town crier" to draw people together and announce the start of the meeting and review the agenda items.

🍄 Have a funny open-ended question at each table that participants must discuss with each other. For example, what does the color purple feel like? If you crossed a penguin and a monkey, what would you call it and what would it look like? If you could add another month to the year, when would you add it and what would you call it? You can also make the questions more pointed and serious, yet still fun, such as "What three things would you change to make work more fun?"

🍄 For smaller groups where there is time to go around and have everyone individually introduce themselves, include some fun information so it's not just an accounting of everyone's "name, rank and serial number." Ask people to share their nickname, how they are feeling on a scale of 1 to 10 or what their job title would be if they named themselves from the perspective of a five-year-old.

🍄 For large gatherings with multiple tables, have fun welcome signs at each table. The signs can serve as a conversation starter and help you divide groups into creative categories for break-out sessions. The possibilities are limitless:

Cat Lovers Here
People Who Love Dilbert Cartoons Here
People with Two Middle Names Here
Avid Golfers Here
People with Unmatched Socks Here
People with Holes in Their Socks Here
Left-Handed People Here
Birthdays in January Here

🍃 Use magnetic poetry kits (which include hundreds of words on tiny magnetic strips) as a conversation starter. You can use the kits as an icebreaker by having people work as a group to put together a poem, vision or "deep thought" related to the meeting based on their random selection of one or two words. (In a creativity workshop I led with the CBC, participants at their leadership retreat used the random magnetic words to develop ideas for a new television show.)

🍃 In large groups, introduce people in bundles to save time and reduce their anxiety about being put on the spot. For example, have everyone stand as a group who traveled more than 6 hours or who have worked for 10 years or more in the company.

Meeting Treasure Hunt Rules

Each participant is given a list of traits they must find in other people. You can do it as a straight list or as a bingo game. Offer a prize for the fastest-completed form. The possibilities for categories are endless and you can customize the hunt to connect it to the theme of the meeting. For example, the "Humor Resources Treasure Hunt" that I use also serves as a springboard for a discussion on several aspects of humor and communication in the workplace. Here are some categories you might use.

Find three people who are from out of province/state.   Find someone who owns a cat.   ➤

Find two people who have a strange hobby.	Find someone with an unusual name.
Find two people who can tell a quick, clean joke.	Find two left-handed people.
Find three people who have worked for the company for more than 10 years.	Find two people who will show you a new dance step.

7. Create Fun Rewards to Promote Good Behavior

Have a cut-out coupon section on your agenda or get folks to toss their names into a hat and offer a door prize at every meeting. They needn't be expensive gifts, perhaps a week's supply of free coffee or a chocolate treat. And use rewards to encourage appropriate meeting behavior. Have a fun prize for whoever utters the most memorable line of the meeting, has the most creative idea, or has the shortest presentation.

8. Use Fun Penalties to Discourage Unwanted Behavior

Have late attendees pay a dollar into the coffee or social fund. Bombard anyone who utters an idea-busting phrase ("we tried that in 1846") with small foam balls. Award an official "foot-in-mouth" award for anyone who says anything considered, by consensus, to be out of line or a personal attack on anyone (a "bonehead prop" that you place over the top of your head like a headband, available at all fine joke shops, is great for this). Play "Jargon Bingo" during meetings to encourage the use of simple language and rid yourselves of the YABA (Yet Another Bloody Acronym) syndrome. Use a buzzer to signal any bad jokes or misfires at humor. And for people whose cell phones go off during a meeting, might I suggest a penalty of $5,000 per call (and yes, this is a pet peeve of mine, why do you ask?). Or simply hand out water pistols to fire at anyone who breaks any of your meeting ground rules.

Meeting Training

Since meetings consume a substantial portion of time and cause loads of stress, review how your meetings are working periodically and offer training in meeting facilitation and conduct. A fun way to pursue this is to develop a fake agenda with humorous topics and assign typical meeting roles for people to role play in an exaggerated manner. Participants could play The Whiner, The Interrupter, The Never-Get-Around-To-Making-a-Clear-Point Guy or The Wisecracker. Videotape the session and then critique the performances and discuss how to deal with these different personalities in a real meeting situation.

9. Hold a Theme Meeting

When I use the phrase "theme day" or "theme meeting," some people invariably roll their eyes and think one of two thoughts: thought #1- "corny"; thought #2 - "Dilbertville has arrived."

When I dig a little deeper into workplace cultures, two things become apparent. In extremely dysfunctional workplaces, adding "theme events" is viewed as the latest ill-conceived attempt to boost morale in the face of other more serious workplace issues. Alternatively, in generally positive workplaces, theme events are not only welcomed, but *they work*. Theme events break people out of their routine, provide folks an opportunity to laugh and unwind a little and encourage a sense of team play. The key to their success is to hold them consistently enough so they become a tradition. If you have regular monthly or weekly meetings, hold a theme meeting every fourth one, or at least a few times a year. The possibilities are limitless. You can tie themes to a holiday (hold a dress-up meeting for Halloween or a gift-exchange meeting at Christmas), or come up with your own variations. Here are a few ideas:

Wacky tie/accessory meeting	Sci-fi theme	International themes
Dress like your co-worker	Western theme	Fashion clashin' day
Beach theme	Dress like your hero	Mismatched socks day
Humor/wacky theme	Polka dot day	Stripes day
Polyester day	50s day	60s day

10. Assign a Meeting Jester

A meeting jester's assignment would include coordinating the food, rewards, celebration plans and any other ideas for livening up a meeting. Keep the jester separate from the chairperson so each of them can attend to their duties properly, but ensure that the jester discusses her or his role and expectations with the facilitator beforehand. If you meet on a regular basis, rotate the responsibility of a "Meeting Jester" around the group.

11. Bring Fun Food

Food can keep energy levels high, serve as an icebreaker and, most importantly, keep people happy. Happy is good. Again, rotate the job of bringing goodies so one or two people don't always carry the burden. Look for unusual food to add more fun. Here are a few suggestions.

🍄 Bring finger foods (cookies in the shape of actual fingers, with blanched almonds for the fingernails).

🍄 Tie the food to a theme. Bring a pie for the budget meeting where you need to slice up the money, lifesavers for the safety meeting, light-bulb-shaped cookies for brainstorming, firm buns to talk about the new company fitness center, waffles to a meeting where no one wants to decide anything, toast for when you want to toast someone and donuts to discuss the new contract with the local police department (I'm kidding!).

🍄 Create your own fortune cookies. There are companies that make customized fortune cookies, or you can bake your own and include thought-provoking or humorous quotes tied to the meeting agenda.

🍄 Popcorn is ideal for meetings where a video presentation is on the agenda.

🍄 Have an "alphabet draw" potluck meeting where you randomly draw a letter, then everyone has to bring a food item starting with that letter.

🍄 Brain food like fresh fruits and low-fat baked goods are ideal for brainstorming meetings where you want everyone's brain fully charged.

🍄 Bring the occasional *really* fun food, like chocolate sundaes, ice cream cones, Jello or lollipops.

12. Get Physical

For meetings longer than 90 minutes, people need to get out of their chairs and move around (which is another reason laughter is a good thing, because it lets people squirm and vibrate in their seats). So plan for a fun way to let people escape from their chairs. Play a theater improv game, run through one of the agenda items with everyone standing, have five minutes of stretching exercises or break for a human resources treasure hunt.

Hop To It!

There are places in Africa where at tribal council meetings, people must stand on one foot while speaking during a meeting. The speaker must stop talking once he puts his foot down. This may be a fun way to keep meetings moving and prevent people from putting their foot in their mouth (or is that where they put the other foot?).

Top Secret Meeting Humor

Rumor has it (this stuff is classified information, so please don't tell anyone) that the late King Hussein of Jordan was a huge fan of AUSTIN POWERS, which he watched while recuperating from an illness in a hospital. During a high-level, big powwow at the U.S. Pentagon, the King supposedly broke into an impersonation of "Dr. Evil" as a way of lightening the mood at the meeting.

13. End on an Upbeat Note

At the end of every morning meeting on the television drama *Hill Street Blues*, Sgt. Phillip Esterhaus stopped everyone as they were getting out of their seats with the same line, week after week: "*Let's be careful out there.*" Wise old Phil had the right idea. A line like this helps end a meeting on a positive note, creates a sense of tradition and lets people know you care about them. Not a bad way to wrap things up. Of course, if you can't come up with a heartfelt, schmaltzy line like Phil (and make it sound sincere to boot), you might want to test drive a few of these oh-so-fun ideas.

Super Meetings!

Some companies believe meetings are so important that they go all out to make an impact. That's why Ernst and Young, a professional services consulting firm, holds its quarterly SuperFriday Meeting Broadcasts. With so many employees on the road the company needs an effective way to reach them. Its solution? A 90-minute live broadcast full of updates and financial reports seasoned heavily with entertainment. The live anything-might-happen-and-sometimes-does broadcasts have included game show-style question and answer sessions for the executives, satirical public service announcements, sketch comedy and lots of self-mocking commentary.

The results? Employees all over the world get updated on company issues, co-workers feel connected to each other and they actually look forward to their next meeting.

- Play music or use a special sound effect that becomes the traditional way to close a meeting.

- End every meeting with a fun door prize(s). The Alberta Business Travelers Association ends their monthly lunch meetings with door prizes donated by their members. They also raise money for their association by charging members a dollar per coupon.

- End with an inspirational or humorous quote or thought of the day.

- Vote on the "most memorable line of the meeting" and reward whoever spoke it.

- End with the humor mill or rumor mill section to get people laughing.

- Go around the table and have everyone list one work-related thing they are most excited about in the upcoming week/month.

Finally, if you are serious about improving your meetings, set aside a few minutes at the end of each meeting to review how it went and to note any suggestions for ways to make the next meeting more effective and fun.

14. Have Great Coffee Available

How can you have a fun, efficient meeting without great coffee? (Okay, so once again, I've arrived at a list with 13 items and needed to stretch it out.)

FINAL AGENDA ITEM

Meetings needn't be onerous, stressful and wasteful. By taking a little time to plan an injection of humor and establishing a relaxed tone throughout, meetings really can be productive, efficient *and fun*.

Meeting adjourned.
And in honor of the late Sgt. Esterhaus, "Let's be humorous out there!"

— 10 —

Speaking of Humor

We've all been there at one time or another, suffering through someone's droning presentation daydreaming about being on a tropical island with Ginger, Mary-Anne or even Gilligan. Sadly, I've heard speeches that were so dry even the presenter fell asleep.

Fortunately, some humor seasoning can add a little zest here and a little zip there to a presentation. Incorporating humor into a presentation doesn't mean you take the topic or audience lightly; on the contrary, it means you know enough about effective communications and respect your audience enough to want to give them a memorable, interesting and dynamic presentation. As Peggy Noonan, presidential speech writer and author of *Simply Speaking* says, "Humor is gracious and shows respect. It shows the audience you think enough of them to want to entertain them."

HUMOR IN ACTION

If you believe that your business presentations are just too important to include humor, consider the following.

☞ A 1984 study by Jones and Vincent on the use of humor in funeral eulogies found that when speakers used generous amounts of heartfelt humor, their credibility rose. The speakers were viewed as a more suitable spokesperson for the deceased.

☂ Clown ministries throughout North America use humor to teach religion.

☂ The Cheers Project uses humor and stand-up comedy to assist people with mental health disabilities.

☂ The Calgary Birth Control Association has used humor, plays and skits to deliver messages about birth control.

☂ The Alberta Committee of Citizens With Disabilities uses fun role plays, props and humor to convey messages about discrimination and living with a disability.

The bottom punchline is this: the more serious or sensitive the presentation topic, the more we may *need* to inject a little fun and humor into our presentation.

> *If we are genuinely interested not just in the transmission of facts and skills, but in the education of the full human being, then we have no choice but to integrate humor into the learning experience.*
> — John Morreall, PhD., Professor of Philosophy

THE CASE FOR ADDING HUMOR TO PRESENTATIONS

Fact #1: You need an audience.

Speaking to a wall has never been a particularly successful way of communicating. If you want to attract an eager audience, then make sure your presentation title and any promotional literature (even if it's just one line in a meeting agenda) convey a sense of fun or enthusiasm. Who wants to go hear Bob spew on about the *Changing Paradigm of Project Management*? Probably only Bob (and even then I wouldn't count on it).

Fact #2: Audiences listen faster than you can say "wake up!"

We live in a world of flippers and zippers. People flip around the TV dial with their remote controls and zip through commercials on their videotapes. The same holds true for members of your audience, except they're channel changing inside their head. The typical business person, according to *Business Week* magazine, has an attention span of only six minutes. And more to the point, while most people speak at an average rate of 150 words per minute, the average listener takes in anywhere from 350 to 600 words per minute. Which means audience members have time to squeeze in other thoughts and still appear to be listening. As you talk, any given audience member may be thinking to themselves, "I wonder what's for lunch?" "I wonder if my wife is still mad at me" or "I wonder what the primary export of Bora Bora is?" Some speakers have suggested that close to two-thirds of an audience in a one-hour presentation will daydream about a sexual fantasy (which is why some audiences actually *want* you to keep speaking longer).

Because of the disparity between speaking and listening rates, audiences need a good "zap" at least once every three to six minutes during a presentation to stay focused and interested. A zap needn't be a song-and-dance number; it may be as simple as slipping in a quote, asking the audience a question or changing the audio-visual medium. Using humor, however, is one of the most effective zaps available. Humor instantly focuses people's attention back to the front of the room and keeps their brains tuned to *your* station.

Fact #3: You must master your nervous energy.

Even the most polished professional speakers admit to getting nervous, and many speakers say they *need* to be nervous in order to be "on." The trick is harnessing that nervous energy and making it work *for* you. Using humor near the start of a presentation helps you breathe easier, relax, slow down and dissipate bottled-up nervous energy. And accessing your sense of humor just prior to presenting does wonders for calming those pre-talk butterflies.

Fact #4: Your audience needs to relax too.

Even audiences get a little anxious, particularly if it's a learning situation. Adding humor helps the audience relax, making them more accepting to new ideas. It also sends the simple but important message: "We're here to have fun too folks!"

Fact #5: Humor helps unite an audience.

A united audience is a good thing (unless they're united against you, but that's a whole other topic), and nothing unites a group of people better than a shared laugh. When people laugh together they are no longer a gaggle of managers or a flock of union workers, but simply a group of human beings with a common reason to smile.

Laughter is a universal uniter.
— Ray Register

Fact #6: Humor helps deliver controversial, authoritative or bad news.

If done effectively, humor can soften bad news. Humor diffuses anxieties, shows concern for the audience and helps people see a bad situation in a more positive light. Studies into the communication of sensitive topics suggest that negative appeals (such as "stop smoking or you might die") have a limited effect, while the use of humor has a much more potent impact. And using humor near the start of a talk can quickly disarm any hostile emotions.

The heaviest moments require the lightest touch.
— Don Ardell

Fact #7: Different people learn in different ways.

Your audience is made up of people who learn in different ways, so to reach everyone effectively, you need to think about incorporating different methods into your presentation. Adding humor is just one more way you can vary your approach.

Fact #8: Humor helps audiences retain information.

Regular bouts of laughter and play boost memory retention. Tapping into audiences' emotions helps them retain information longer and remember the ideas hidden inside the humor. One study found that students who took a university statistics course with humor sprinkled into the lectures scored 15% higher on exams than their non-humored counterparts. Another study showed that "concept humor"—humor related to the topic – significantly improved information retention.

Fact #9: Humor improves your credibility and builds rapport.

Credibility and likeability contribute to the overall success of the delivery of any message. If you are going to persuade an audience, then first and foremost they have to trust and like you. Humor is a perfect way to build trust, reduce the distance between a speaker and the audience and reduce the authoritativeness of the presenter. Humor can convey the notion that you are "all in this together" and that the presenter shares some of the same experiences. Finding common ground with humor allows a speaker to meet an audience where they are at. In fact, studies have linked humor with a speaker's credibility, appeal, intelligence, audience attention, participation, retention, comprehension and attitudinal changes. And the use of humorous satire has been shown to substantially improve the persuasiveness of the arguments presented.

> *If you are going to tell people the truth, you'd better make them laugh. Otherwise they'll kill you.*
> — George Bernard Shaw

Fact #10: Humor helps you have fun too.

Adding humor ensures that you don't get bored with the material either. If you're delivering the same talk for the 18th time, or delivering a talk on a dry topic, then you need to think about making it fun for your sake as well. After all, if you can't get enthusiastic about your topic, why on earth would you expect anyone in your audience to care about it? Using humor can keep the material fresh and lively, and help you look forward to your next presentation.

> *No one ever sold anybody anything by boring them to death.*
> — David Ogilvy, ad man

Fact #11: Humor can make complex topics less intimidating.

Let's face it, some topics are downright scary. Humor once again rides to the rescue by making even the most frightening topics less scary and easier to understand. Using humor in dry topics has an even greater impact than using it with topics already perceived as interesting. And using humor to deliver sensitive topics can help people confront the material by allowing them to laugh at it.

Fact #12: Humor can reinforce your message.

Jokes and funny anecdotes can help you reiterate your main points in small, easy to digest chunks, allowing you to repeat your main message in a varied and lighthearted manner.

Humor is the lubricant that can make a message go down smoother.

— Michael Jeffreys, professional speaker

Fact #13: **Humor changes perspectives**.

Because humor involves a twist in logic, using it can change an audience's perspective on an issue. And since we know humor is a catalyst for creative thinking, it also helps to open up minds and encourage more flexible attitudes.

Fact #14: **Humor can leave people feeling positive**.

Ideally, you want your audience going away feeling positive about you, the talk and themselves. Humor helps foster an upbeat tone that leaves people in a positive mood.

Fact #15: **Humor keeps us humble**.

One of the few speaking sins that an audience just won't forgive is when presenters take themselves too seriously. Self-effacing humor keeps speakers humble and accessible to the audience and helps them to recover graciously from bloopers (which are bound to happen anytime we open our mouths in front of a large group of people).

There you have it. Fifteen compelling reasons to take humor seriously the next time you speak. Let's have a look now at some specific ways you can sprinkle a bit of humor into your next presentation.

ADDING HUMOR TO YOUR NEXT PRESENTATION (OR THE ONE AFTER THAT)

Recovering From Speaking Blunders

If you trip up while speaking in public, it's important to laugh at yourself (when speaking in private to yourself, it's less critical). Laughing relaxes both the presenter and the audience, while ignoring a blooper sometimes causes the speaker and the audience to get nervous. Remember, by laughing at yourself, you ensure the audience is on your side and laughing *with* you, not at you. The trick is to laugh at yourself without putting yourself down or causing the audience to lose faith in your credentials.

To help blooper-proof a presentation, you can prepare standard recovery lines for virtually any speaking blunder. And better yet, tailor the lines to your specific audience or topic whenever possible. Here are a few standard, all-purpose recovery lines for some common speaking blunders.

Problem	Response
Losing your place	"Sorry, my hard drive just crashed." "I think I lost my place, can anyone find it out there?" "Does anyone know what I was about to say next?"
Speaker/microphone feedback	"Wow, was it something I said?" "Everyone has an opinion on this matter." "I haven't had this much static since . . ." "Wow, built-in sound effects."
Lights go out momentarily	"Wow, was it good for you too?" "Was it something I said?" "All right, whose turn was it to pay the electrical bill?"
Bulb burns out on a projector	"Is there a technician in the house?" "We are experiencing some technical difficulties, please do not adjust your set." "Houston . . . we have a problem."
Dropping your notes	"Thank you, thank you, a standing ovation please." "And now for my encore, I'll do a half gainer off the podium." "And now you know why I was always picked last on the baseball team."
Checking/rechecking a microphone	"Can you hear me at the back? Do you *want* to hear me at the back?"
Tripping	"You know folks, any *ordinary* person would have fallen completely over." "Never try that at home kids." "Wow – a perfect 10 from the Romanian judge."
Tongue-tied	"Did you understand that? Because I sure didn't!" "Sorry, I just had a new tongue installed this morning." "Does anyone have some scissors so I can untie my tongue?"
Voice cracks	"And now you know what singing whales sound like." "I'm a late bloomer . . . I just started puberty half an hour ago." "Is this an early sign I'm beginning to crack up?"
No one responds when you prompt the audience with a question	"Well, there goes the free trip to Hawaii." "Perhaps I should rephrase the question in English." "Does anyone want to use a lifeline?"

No one responds when you ask the audience if they have any questions	"How about any questions about where I buy my clothes?" "I know the first question is the hardest, so let's move on to the last question." "Well, either I've answered all your questions or I've confused the heck out of you."
When a joke falls flat	"I'm pretty much just amusing myself at this point." "Boy, and I thought Saskatchewan was flat." "I've often wondered, if a joke falls flat in the forest . . . then I guess you wouldn't hear any laughter there either." "Thank you for holding your laughter until I say something that is actually funny." "I think that one was written by (put in name of the audience's competitor)."
Stumbling over the pronunciation of a word	Try to say the term two or three times, then finally replace it with a simpler word or phrase (e.g., "ornigal, er, ornithologoist, er . . . bird expert") "Or as we say in English . . . (repeat the correct pronunciation)" "Or, as I like to say . . . (repeat correct word)."
Slides or overheads are out of focus	"Am I in focus, at least?" "Oops, I was heavily sedated when I took this one." "My point here is simple—I think our (your) company needs to be more focused."
Being heckled	"Thanks for your help, but I usually work alone." "Please let's hold all heckling until after the program so you'll have even more material." "Wow, that's the first time I've heard feedback from the sound system sound like an actual person."
Cell phone goes off in the audience	"I'm busy right now, can you take a message?" "If it's Mom, tell her I'll call her tomorrow." "If it's Revenue Canada/the IRS/the CIA/the police, I'm not here." (in a whispered voice)

Did You Hear the One . . . ?

My way of joking is to tell the truth. It's the funniest joke in the world.

— George Bernard Shaw

Jokes, as I'll get to shortly, are only one of many ways to add a touch of humor to a presentation.

An effectively delivered joke can convey a powerful or insightful thought wrapped up in a small, humorous nugget. To be truly effective at using jokes in a presentation, you need to consider a few simple guidelines.

1. Use fresh jokes only. Old jokes sound canned (which is probably where they belong) and chances are some of the audience has heard them before. Humor needs an element of surprise to work, which makes old jokes ineffective. So forget about the joke Uncle Vinnie told you 12 years ago or even last summer. Most jokes have a fairly short expiration date (now there's an idea, why don't jokes come with expiration dates?

"Hey Brian, how did that last joke go over with the audience?

You know, like a little warning label: "This joke best told before August 4, 2002"). Even comedian Jerry Seinfeld recently retired a few hours worth of old jokes as a way to force himself to freshen up his act. And besides the joke itself becoming old, the language or ideas behind a joke also become dated. The safest way to make sure a joke is fresh is to write it yourself.

Be careful, however, of telling a new, never-before-tested joke near the start of a presentation. If it bombs, it could cause you to lose credibility and increase your anxiety, the opposite of the desired effect! So try out new material later during a talk, once you've won the audience over and are feeling at ease and in command of your presentation.

2. Off-color jokes are off limits. Because so many jokes fall into the category of "off-color," if you use a joke pay extra attention to make sure the humor is safe. Racist, sexist, ethnic, political and any discriminatory jokes are off limits. And ensure there is no vulgar language in the joke. If there is even a chance of offending one person, find another joke. A great guideline for judging a joke is to pretend your mother, your aunt (the nun) or your grandmother is in the audience. In the front row. With her hearing aid on.

3. Tell relevant jokes, which preferably link to a message. As Canadian comedian Steve Smith (a.k.a. "Red Green") reminds us, "Comedy is the courier, not the package." Whenever possible, there should be a reason for telling a joke; never tell a joke just for the sake of getting a laugh. Humor in a talk should adhere to the "killing two birds with one stone" rule. In addition to the chuckles, there should be a point tied to the joke. Any joke should connect either to you, the audience, the location you are speaking in or, preferably, the subject matter of your presentation. It's sometimes easy to change characteristics within a joke so it becomes more relevant. Instead of saying "two guys go into a bar," change it to "two ACME financial planners go into a bar . . ."

Practicing related humor also strengthens the presenter's appeal, according to a study by Zillman and Bryant. They compared the nature of humor used in university lectures, and found that the instructor's appeal significantly increased when humor was connected to the subject matter.

The easiest way to gather relevant material is to start collecting funny stories, top-10 lists, jokes, strange terms and bloopers for each topic you speak on and put them into a humor file.

4. Keep jokes short and to the point. One of the advantages of jokes over anecdotes is that they can deliver big messages in small packages, so ideally the shorter the joke the better. Shorter jokes are also easier to memorize and don't require as big a payoff in the punchline. Remember the longer the set-up portion of your joke, the greater the surprise has to be in the punchline in order to get a laugh.

5. Practice, practice, practice. Everyone can tell a joke; few can tell a joke well. Joke telling is an art form, so *practice*. Try out potential jokes on safe guinea pigs, like family members, co-workers or friends (keeping in mind they are biased and might laugh themselves silly because they want to be included in your will). Here are few joke delivery and writing points to ponder.

🍸 A joke that is meant to be only 12 words long can die a slow, torturous death when stretched out to 30 words, so make every word and every nuance count.

🍸 Practice the timing. As comedian Jack Benny said, "Timing isn't knowing so much when to speak . . . it's knowing when to pause." Know where an effective pause should be placed to deliver the greatest oomph (usually, though not always, just before the punchline). And be sure to pause after the delivery of a joke so you don't speak over the thunderous laughter.

🍸 The joke should blend seamlessly into the fabric of your presentation. Edit out extraneous comments or unnecessary set-ups that weaken a joke and raise false expectations. Avoid comments like, "Now I'd like to tell a funny joke . . ." or "Something really funny happened to me that I'd like to share with you . . ."

🍄 Use specific language. For example, when telling a joke that includes automobiles, don't just say "car," say "my blue Volkswagen Beetle." Painting a clearer picture helps people to better visualize a joke.

🍄 Choose words carefully. Some words sound funnier than others. Back of the throat sounds, like a hard "g" or "k," are funnier (because they are less common) than front of the throat sounds. So, in theory, duck and muck are funnier than swan or mud. (Trust me on this, I'm a professional.)

🍄 Practice punching different key words to see what sounds best. Usually descriptive adjectives or nouns need a little extra energy or volume.

🍄 Your gestures, facial expressions and tone of voice should mirror the delivery of a good joke. The delivery should also be as conversational in tone as possible. Depending on the type of joke, deadpanning the delivery is often the best approach, especially during the set-up portion; with some jokes, though, you may need to play the ham and exaggerate gestures and vocal tones.

🍄 As a general rule, the punchline should be delivered with a little more volume and energy than the set-up portion of the joke.

🍄 Many humorists believe that when you deliver the punchline you should sustain eye contact with a receptive member of the audience as though you are delivering it personally to that particular person.

6. Think about placement in the talk. You need to decide where the joke will be most effective.

Be careful, for example, of the "I-need-an-opening-joke" syndrome. Jokes at the very beginning of a talk can sometimes come across as contrived and forced. They can, however, be used to introduce a new segment of a talk, as a segue between sections or to summarize a point. But don't overdo the frequency of jokes, or any other humor. For the incongruity of humor to work, you need to return to reality now and then. Think of jokes as a seasoning designed to add a little zest here and there without overpowering the flavor of your presentation. (Incidentally, the world joke-telling records belong to a Peruvian who launched 345 jokes over one hour, and an Ohio man who delivered 12,682 jokes over a 24-hour period. Now *that's* overkill.)

7. Have a Recovery Plan. Johnny Carson was (as David Letterman is now) a master at recovering from "the bomb," usually getting greater guffaws from the postmortem on a deceased punchline than from the actual joke itself. So plan a recovery if a joke doesn't work (see Recovering From Speaker Blunders), and tie it to the topic or audience whenever possible. And never repeat or explain a bombed joke, simply move on. Explaining a misfired joke will prolong the agony and lower your credibility. If the joke is so well-crafted that it delivers a message in addition to the humor, then all is not necessarily lost if the joke fails to get any laughs.

If you don't get a great laugh the first time out, don't give up on a joke prematurely. The joke may have failed for all sorts of reasons, including the phase of the moon, so try it at least two or three times and experiment with the delivery before declaring it officially dead.

Finally, be cautious about judging all of your humor on the basis of laughter. Certain nationalities, cultures and even certain organizational cultures don't foster a climate of expressive laughers. Some folks just aren't very demonstrative in public. Men, for example, tend to laugh less openly in groups than women. (A study by Robert Provine, MD, suggests that women laugh 126% more often than men – males are more apt to be "laugh-getters" than laughers.) I've had men who sat through an entire program stone-faced, then told me afterwards how hilarious they thought it was (which always leads me to think, "Would it have killed you to crack a smile?"). An audience full of strangers will typically laugh less than audiences who know each other. So beware of using laughter as the *only* measure of success; sometimes all you should aim for are smiles (and trust me, smiles in an audience beat scowls hands down every time).

> *There are things of deadly earnest that can only be
> mentioned under the cover of a joke.*
> — J.J. Procter

Is It Time to Laugh?

Many factors influence how openly an audience laughs. Because laughter is so contagious, smaller groups typically laugh less than larger audiences. Seating arrangements can serve to stifle or encourage laughter. In general, classroom-style seating suppresses laughter, while auditorium and, better yet, circular seating, where audience members can all see each other are more conducive to laughter.

Time of day can have a huge impact on laughter. Some humorists suggest it's harder to get laughs early in the morning because people are still sleepy and aren't programmed to laugh then. (Even the wacky flight attendants at Southwest Airlines realize that early morning flights aren't the best time to be cracking lots of jokes over the PA system.) Lunch talks often generate easier laughs, when audiences are desperate for some relief during a long day, whereas late afternoons are another tough time for generating laughter. After-dinner talks should incorporate more humor because most audiences, by the end of the day, are overloaded on information and want to be entertained. Moreover, because they are tired and restless, they need to laugh as an excuse for moving around in their seats.

To Laugh or Not to Laugh? That is the Question

I'm often asked if it's okay to laugh after you deliver a joke or have told a funny story. There are no hard and fast rules. It depends on the nature of the humor, your style and, literally, the moment. As a very general guideline, I'd say that most jokes are better delivered without the presenter laughing, especially during the set-up part of the joke. The more deadpan you deliver the lead-in, the greater the surprise when the punchline hits the audience. But there's always exceptions.

Phyllis Diller, the first famous female stand-up comedian, laughed at all her own jokes, despite being told doing so was a big no-no. She persisted and her unique laugh became part of her trademark. People responded positively to her laugh because it seemed natural and genuine, which is the most important rule in all of this. If your laugh comes from the heart and is genuine and spontaneous, then you can't go wrong.

Some funny stories work best with an animated face and even laughing along the way to help generate momentum for laughter. Depending on the story, the audience may even *need* to hear you laugh to know this *is* a funny story, and that *yes*, it's okay to laugh even though you're telling a somewhat tragic tale. Your facial expressions, tone of voice, body language and your own laughter are highly contagious and can act as an early warning signal that laughter is strongly encouraged.

Why Anecdotes are the Best Antidote Against Boredom

If you carefully follow the brilliant words of advice I've offered above, then jokes can be a wonderful way to add some humor seasoning to your talk. Given a choice, however, between a joke and funny story, funny anecdotes win, in my books, hands down. Here's why.

Jokes vs.	Humorous anecdotes
Rely heavily on memory; can be easily forgotten.	Since they're your own stories, you won't get lost or forget them.
May be outdated; always a chance the audience will have heard them before.	Audience won't have heard them (unless they live with you).
Depend heavily on timing and perfect delivery.	Less reliant on delivery, more dependent on content.
Some jokes risk offending people.	Low chance to offend.
Depend on audience "getting it."	Less investment required by audience.
Because audience know it's a joke, the set-up requires a big "payoff" in the punchline to get a good laugh.	Less set-up than a joke, so it's usually easier to get several laughs with a good story.
Often hard to find jokes that link to the audience or talk topic.	Easier to make a connection to the topic, to illustrate a point or use as an example.
Harder to deliver with authenticity (although the delivery will vary, anyone can tell the same joke).	Because they're your stories, it strengthens your authenticity; helps separate you from other speakers (no one else can tell your stories, you own them).
Harder for audience to digest content associated with joke.	People communicate via stories, stories are how we best remember & store information.

Now, having said all that (and even put in a table, for goodness sakes), you probably think I'm anti-joke. Not at all. I often tell jokes in talks and have performed stand-up comedy. I love jokes (that's why I spent all that time coaching you on how to tell them properly). However, I write my own jokes and test-drive them dozens of times before they see the light of day. Rather than advocating a boycott on jokes, I'm simply suggesting that humorous stories are often overlooked and are usually a much more powerful form of communication and humor.

Humorous anecdotes are the perfect snooze antidote for any type of business presentation, regardless of the formality of the situation. People love stories. Stories bring dry material to life and make information relevant and more meaningful for people. Stories have always been, and continue to be, the primary way people communicate. When we come home at the end of a work day, I'm certain most of us don't pull out a flip chart or hand out pie charts to explain how our day went. So use stories, especially your own, to connect with the audience's heart and their funny bone.

You don't need to look far for funny stories. Everyone has lived them. Scour your childhood experiences, early college days and work experiences for funny anecdotes that have a message relevant to your talk. And remember, often your funniest stories are born out of your worst pain.

A way to incorporate safe, self-effacing humor is to share your early mishaps about the topic at hand. These stories can help your audience feel less intimidated about the topic knowing you were once at the level where they may be today. For example, when I talk about public speaking skills, I open with a story about one of my early speaking disasters, when I was so nervous my leg shook like Elvis on steroids. The story always gets a laugh and lets the audience know that I really do know what it's like to be nervous about the prospect of public speaking.

> *Funny tales are the best. It is comedy that binds humanity together.*
> — Lord Ashley Allison

Self-effacing Humor

The safest form of humor is laughing at yourself. Self-effacing humor sends the message to your audience that you are *so* confident, you can even poke fun at yourself. Canadian politicians (like Preston Manning mocking the way he said Refor-r-r-rm) who clamber to get on the comedy show *This Hour Has 22 Minutes* certainly realize the beneficial optics of laughing at themselves. Former U.S. President Ronald Reagan constantly poked fun at his age, while former Vice President Al Gore joked about his own wooden personality. Be wary though, of using put-down humor directed at your own talk.

Real Life, Real Humor

Scott Adams, the creator of Dilbert, gets approximately 800 real-life experience e-mails each and every day, which he claims form the basis for most of his cartoons. Bob Newhart, in an interview in LAUGHING MATTERS, tell us: "What comedians do – we look at your world and say 'Don't you realize how really strange your world is?' We comedians watch you, and then we do you, and then you pay to watch us do you.'" In other words, when you are going on a humor hunt for potential stories – real life really is stranger, and much funnier, than fiction.

The absolute truth is the thing that makes people laugh.
— Carl Reiner

Comments like "For those of you still awake" or "Gee, I wish I had spent more than five minutes preparing this speech" won't do you any service; they simply reflect a lack of respect for your audience.

Steve Ballmer, chief executive for Microsoft, practiced some effective self-effacing humor at a computer trade show. The presentation included a parody of *Austin Powers* (complete with Dr. Evil and "Austin Gates"), a spoof of the television show *Judge Judy* and even some jokes about common computer glitches that Microsoft is known for.

During his last address at the White House Correspondents' dinner, U.S. President Bill Clinton also took the opportunity to provide a few yuk yuks at his own expense. "In just eight years I've given you enough material for twenty," Clinton quipped. He went on to tell the 2,600 member audience that his career objective was "to remain president." The highlight of the evening was a video that parodies Clinton's last few months in office as a "lame duck president." The video showed Clinton practicing his golf swing, making lunches for wife Hillary and holding press conferences in front of a lone, sleeping journalist. While his speech illustrated how effective self-effacing humor is, it also provided an example of the fine humor line we sometimes walk. Although Clinton scored big points for his comedic timing and humility, some journalists pondered a bigger question about the line between entertainment and competent leadership skills. The issue for these journalists boiled down to this: "Should presidents be signing up for stand-up comedy training or, worse, hired for their comedic abilities?" My answer to this dilemma is, "No . . . but it might help."

OTHER HUMOR SOURCES AND TYPES

The fun doesn't end with jokes and funny anecdotes. With a little imagination there are dozens of ways to add the humor ingredient to your next business presentation (or the one after that).

🍷 Introductions. There are many humorous ways to open a talk, from funny quotes to offering up an amazing, yet bizarre statistic. Although you should tailor your introduction to the audience, you can also write a standard humorous introductory line that's good for any talk. American politician Bob Dole once opened with, "That introduction was the most recent one I've had." Or you might try, "I know you were looking forward to someone who was witty, handsome, eloquent, well-dressed and charming . . . (pause) unfortunately he couldn't make it."

🍷 Inside humor. Asking audience members before a presentation for examples of "inside" humor is a sure-fire way to score points and practice relevant humor. Inside humor is not only more powerful, it impresses the audience by showing them you've done your homework.

🍷 Props. Look for strange props, posters or costume items that will add some fun and tie into your message. People are primarily visual learners, so adding fun props will also help them retain the information. Some props can even be used by entire audiences. For example, handing out noisemakers or cheerleader pompoms to members of the audience and then instructing them on their use during a talk is an easy way to inject some fun.

You don't have to hunt far for props. With a little creativity, everyday household items can convey all sorts of messages. Use a beach towel to show how you're not throwing in the towel, a handful of loose change to talk about how much change has been happening or a boomerang to highlight how you want customers coming back after you send them out of the store.

🍄 Fun videos. With a little imagination, video clips (be careful of copyright violations) or your own in-house productions can add a little humor.

🍄 Sound effects. Bring a small portable stereo to add some funny sound effects or music appropriate to the occasion. For example, if you are talking about phasing out an old computer system, you might play a somber funeral march, then play pomp and circumstance music to introduce the new software.

🍄 Overhead/slide presentations. Throw in something totally irrelevant in the middle of a set of serious images, like a picture of your dog, a pie chart showing the consumption rates of pie in Canada or the latest hockey statistics. Although this breaks the rule of making humor relevant, sometimes a comic detour is the perfect technique to keep an audience on their toes and interject a laugh when they really need it. You can also use funny drawings or cartoons to illustrate a point (again, be careful of copyright violations—it's not ethical or legal to show those *Dilbert* cartoons without permission) or add funny quotes that serve as a caption for each new section or slide of your talk. And with current technology, it's easier than ever to incorporate fun photos of your audience right in a slide production.

🍄 Spontaneous moments. Take advantage of spontaneous moments, including bloopers, or audience comments, to add some fun. Spontaneity adds to your credibility, makes the presentation more fresh and lets the audience know you are truly engaged in your talk.

🍄 Exaggeration. Exaggeration is a common source of humor, so look for opportunities to use it to write new jokes or embellish a great anecdote.

🍄 Marry unrelated ideas or create a humorous metaphor. Making a connection between motivating employees and training your dog or relating how marketing to new customers was like courting your spouse illustrates how marrying unrelated ideas can lead to humor. Simply look at your topic and ask yourself, "how is _____ similar to _____"; then randomly substitute different words or ideas until something makes sense in a humorous sort of way.

🍄 Reverse gears. A common form of humor is simply to look at an issue or topic from the completely opposite perspective. If, for example, you are speaking on teambuilding, provide information on how to help really nice people to not get along with each other.

🍄 Parody. Although blatantly stealing or borrowing something from another source is an infringement of copyright laws, parodying an object or idea is permissible. You can use parody, for example, to mimic books like the *Chicken Soup for the Soul* series or to spoof David Letterman's talk show.

🍄 Rule of threes. Educators, writers and speakers often talk of how many things are best packaged in "threes". This truism applies to humor as well, by allowing you to establish a pattern in a list with the first two items, then to throw in a monkey wrench for the third item. For example, "The three things you need to carry when hiking are rain gear, extra food, and . . . someone who knows the way."

🍄 Quotes. Many excellent quotation books are available. You can also collect humorous quotes from articles, newspapers, movies, television shows and even family members, or alter commonly known quotes, for example, "too err is humor." The shorter and punchier the quote, the better. For the best oomph, always provide the source of the quote first, then the actual quote. For example, "As George Burns always said, 'It's easy to ad lib if you've got it written down.'"

🍄 Trivia. Using obscure or bizarre statistics or trivia is an easy way to add a little humor. For example, when I speak on the Canadian Rockies, I sprinkle in strange little facts such as how Banff is the "elevator capital of Canada" or how there is a crater on Mars named after Banff.

🍄 Top-10 lists. At the computer software company PeopleSoft in California, the CEO does a top-10 list at every quarterly meeting. Any topic lends itself to a top-10 list. You can either make a completely silly one or combine serious information with a sprinkling of wacky tidbits. The shorter and snappier you can make the 10 items, the better. The possibilities are limitless, for example: "The Top 10 Reasons You Should Care About _____"; "The Top 10 Reasons Our Customers Love Us" or "The Top 10 Signs We Need to Upgrade Our Computer System."

- Create a "What's In and What's Out" list. Lists like this, that spoof fashion articles are an easy recipe for humor that can be applied to any topic.

- Create a "Good News and Bad News" list. Again, this type of list is a standard comic formula for generating laughs.

- Throw things (preferably soft things) at the audience. Tossing out hats, paper airplanes or chocolate treats is an easy way to generate some fun. When I talk about the need to spread humor in the workplace, I often toss clown noses into the audience as fun keepsakes.

- Repetition. Repeating a shocking statement or amazing statistic over and over and over, to the point of silliness, can sometimes be a funny way of making a memorable point.

- Funny surveys. Survey the audience on a funny topic, then use the survey as a springboard to talk about a serious message. Or find humorous surveys related to the topic. When speaking recently to a business travel organization, I mentioned a survey that suggested the number one item business travelers wanted to take home with them from the hotel was – the housekeeper.

- Humor in handouts. Don't forget to include humor in any handouts or reference material you pass out to the audience. Using cartoons, funny headings, audience members' names, humorous quotes or some lively clip art can lighten up any type of printed material.

- Funny words. Look for industry-related terms or acronyms you can poke fun at or come up with an alternative meaning for.

- Poke fun at the boss. The next best thing to poking fun at yourself is poking fun at the boss. (Just get the boss's permission first!)

- Plant questions or hecklers. Humor can be generated by planting some fun pre-planned questions in the audience. I've had audience members call me on their cell phone to get a few laughs.

- Incorporate magic. For a relatively low cost, most joke stores offer simple magic tricks that anyone can easily learn. (Magic has become such a hit that one New York consultant charges $1,000 per hour to teach business executives a little magic for their next presentation.)

🍄 This day in history. Often, a humorous opening can be found by searching for significant, yet humorous events that happened on the day of your presentation.

🍄 The "old bait and switch" routine. This is another standard fare of comics. It involves setting up a statement or question to make the answer seem obvious, then finishing the statement with the opposite or an unexpected answer. When I spoke in Waterton Lakes National Park, I opened with: "I'm so excited to be here in Waterton. I know you probably won't believe me, you'll probably think I'm just saying this, but of ALL the national parks in Canada . . . Jasper is my favorite." Naturally, the audience thought I was going to say Waterton (the bait); Jasper was the switch. I heard a WestJet flight attendant use this strategy when, during the introduction of their safety regulations talk, she said, "And if you would please pay attention to the demonstration at the front of the plane . . . I'd be really surprised."

🍄 Role plays. Using audience volunteers to role play a sales situation or customer complaint always generates some laughter.

🍄 Games or quizzes. Incorporating a game show-style quiz segment and hamming up the host role is a reliable way to engage an audience and add humor.

🍄 Door prizes. Door prizes are a simple way to add some fun. Ideally, make the prizes relevant to your talk or message.

🍄 Word play. Victor Hugo once said, "Puns are the guano of the winged mind." Puns, thought by many to be the "lowest form of humor," are the most basic form of word play. My advice is if a pun happens spontaneously, go for it. Otherwise, avoid them. Malapropisms are humorous misuses of similar sounding words that result in a rather silly effect, such as saying condom instead of condiment. Spoonerisms are named for William A. Spooner, the former Oxford dean who made them famous. A spoonerism (the technical term is "metaphasis") occurs when the front letters of two words are transposed, resulting in a humorous alternative meaning. One of Spooner's most famous spoonerisms was "queer old dean" in place of "dear old queen." Again, when they happen spontaneously, spoonerisms are great laugh generators.

🍄 Terms of vernacular. In the animal world there are gaggles of geese, sloths of bears, knots of toads and parliaments of owls. For a little humor, try applying terms of vernacular like these to the audience. For example, you might welcome a summation of accountants, a forest of foresters, a litigation of lawyers or a storm of meteorologists.

T Location humor. Look for humor related to the geographic location, room or building you are speaking in, but be careful not to offend anyone when speaking on someone else's turf. If you are speaking in a small town, refer to it as the gateway to an even smaller town nearby, or refer to a famous city as the gateway to an obscure nearby town. Scan the daily newspaper for wacky local headlines, or see if there's anything in the weather worth laughing about. Just be careful of using any put-down humor about an audience's hometown – folks tend to get very defensive about their homes.

T Weather humor. Sharing humorous observations or jokes about the weather is a favorite pastime for many folks that has probably been going on since the first public talk.

CLOSING THOUGHTS

Take the time to inject some humor into your next presentation. Just make sure the humor is safe, relevant to the topic and authentic to your own style (although as George Burns once advised, "If you can fake sincerity, you've got it made."). Even if you don't get the laughs you hoped for the first time out, your audience will appreciate any sincere attempt you make to liven up the presentation.

— 11 —

Humor Blocks

Teaching a person to develop a sense of humor who has a lot of inhibitions is like flushing a drain which is blocked with rubble. Once you remove the blockade, water will start flowing.

Dr. Madan Kataria, Laughter Club Founder

It's worth taking a bit of a detour to explore what blocks our access to our humor resources. What leads to osteoporosis of the funny bone? What makes it difficult to practice humor in the workplace at both an individual and an organizational level?

INDIVIDUAL HUMOR BLOCKS

You have to admit it's difficult to find somber, overly serious four-year-olds who take themselves too seriously. In the preschool next to my office, you'll seldom find a child standing off to the side saying, "I'm not going to participate in this silly exercise because I'm a little worried about what my peers will think and how this will effect my image as I embark on my kindergarten education." Instead, you find a group of constantly imaginative, creative, curious and playful people (albeit very small people). Their world is full of possibilities. They can find pleasure and play in the simplest

> *Nothing, no experience good or bad, no belief, no cause, is in itself momentous enough to monopolize the whole of life to the exclusion of laughter.*
> — Alfred North Whitehead

The Laughter Deficit

The average five-year-old laughs 300 to 400 or more times a day, while the average adult laughs 15 times a day or less. This seems very unbalanced and very unfair, so I think adults should take a cue from children and start laughing a lot more. Either that, or we have to start making our children's lives a lot more miserable, because something sure seems out of whack.

> *Humorists always sit at the children's table.*
> — Woody Allen

of moments (in fact, I don't know why parents spend so much money on toys; when I was a child I played with dirt). These children wouldn't know how to take themselves seriously if they tried. So what happens?

What happens is as we grow up, we get told a countless number of times to do just that – "grow up!" And act your age. And quit being silly. And get to work. And we get told to never mix business with

"I AM smiling."

pleasure, leading some to mistakenly believe that work is not a time for play or fun. Indeed, many view work and play as polar opposites, and because we feel the workplace is off limits to any sort of play, we save fun for our off-work hours. And before long we get swept into the rat race, forgetting the words of Lily Tomlin, "Even if you win the rat race, you are still a rat." Sure the boss throws us the odd piece of cheese, but for the most part we wait to have fun. We wait for the end of the workday. We wait for the weekend. We wait for vacation. Some of us even wait for retirement before the fun kicks in.

Of course, the solution to getting out of the rat race and re-entering the human race, which I've preached throughout this book (you *have* been reading the book, haven't you?), is to mix copious amounts of fun and humor into your work life. Which means, as a starting point, tapping into that five-year-old buried inside you. But why *do* we block access to our five-year-old self? Have a look at the following humor blocks and see if they ring any serious alarm bells.

1. I'm Too Professional to Laugh. We covered this in chapter 1, so go back and re-read it if you are still suffering from professionalitis. Here's the recap: using humor at work is about taking *ourselves* lightly, not our jobs.

2. I'm Too Old to Have Fun. Ever heard of someone named George Burns? Our sense of humor doesn't come with an expiry date. As Michael Pritchard said, "You don't stop laughing because you grow old; you grow old because you stop laughing." Or as someone equally sage said, "Age is only important if you are cheese or wine."

3. I'm Too Sexy to Laugh. Some people believe it's just not sexy to laugh or have fun. Yet, 98% of women surveyed in France would rather have a lover with a great sense of humor than someone with a great body. And correct me if I'm wrong, but French women know what's sexy.

4. I'm Too Cool to Laugh. This condition is prevalent in teenagers, when it's no longer cool to laugh at certain things, particularly themselves. Some of this attitude spills over into adulthood, where people believe it's cool to be as cool as a cucumber and keep their emotions in check. Let's face it, we don't often see James Bond giggling or playing with a Slinky.

5. I'm Too Macho to Laugh. I've noticed that when my audience is 50% or more women, the laughs tend to come a little easier. Other humorists agree with me on this. Men tend to laugh once they have the okay from other men to laugh (the other men presumably being wimps). This may stem from the idea that showing emotions openly is a feminine trait, not appropriate for boys and men unless it's a put-down style of humor. American psychologist David Dodd analyzed over 15,000 yearbook photos and found that even when it comes to just smiling, let alone laughing out loud, girls out smile boys by a wide margin. Dodd found no gender difference in kindergarten, but by grades 4 to 6 males start to look grimmer, and by junior high the gender difference is obvious. Dodd also found differences in adults, where, he suggests, men try to look serious "to prove they are men," while women tend to smile more to make other people around them relax. Dodd and I may be grossly over generalizing here, but there is a certain amount of truth to the "I'm too macho to laugh" humor block.

6. I'm Too Tired to Laugh. Obviously your physical state can have a huge impact on your ability to access your humor. If you are tired, physically drained, stressed to the max or just plain sick, it's hard to tickle the old funny bone. So watch two comedies and get to bed early tonight.

7. I'm Too Perfect to Laugh. Research into play suggests that egos are a major humor block. Expressing your sense of humor involves taking a bit of a risk. What if no one laughs? What if my funny overture goes unappreciated? If we are perfectionists who like to be constantly in control, this could cause hardening of the laugh arteries. And, because perfectionists tend to stress out and beat themselves up when things go even slightly wrong, they have a tougher time accessing their humor during mishaps. If you suffer from this ailment, keep the words of Richard Carlson, author of *Don't Sweat the Small Stuff at Work*, in mind: "When you leave room in your heart for errors, you also leave room in your heart for humor."

8. I Don't Have Time to Laugh. In this fast-paced, busy, busy, oh-so-busy world, we sometimes don't make the time to laugh as often as we need to. I've met people who feel they cannot indulge in even a two-minute chuckle-fest for fear that they'll lag behind in the old rat race. If you catch yourself thinking you can't afford the time to laugh, remind yourself of just the opposite: that given all the benefits of humor, you can't afford *not* to take the time to laugh.

9. I'm Afraid of Being Embarrassed. Three-year-old children don't embarrass easily; they *learn* to embarrass easily as they grow up. I've said it before, and I'll say it here again in case you missed it (it's not that I don't trust you, I just want to make sure you understand this critical point): when you learn to laugh at yourself and your own foibles, you take away everyone's ability to laugh at you. Of course there are still times when we feel embarrassed, but beating people to the punchline is a sure-fire recipe for minimizing your own discomfort in many of life's awkward moments.

Some folks are even embarrassed about how their laugh sounds, so they tend to keep it bottled up inside. This is truly a shame, since unique, colorful laughs often generate even more group laughter (just ask my friend, "the snorter"). Laughter is simply too precious a gift to keep hidden inside.

> *Laugh at yourself before anyone else can.*
> — Elsa Maxwell

10. I'm Not Listening. Poor listening skills are a common humor block. Ditto for not being observant. When you aren't tuned in to what's going on around you, you can miss out on a lot of humor. The more you open your eyes, ears and mind, the more humor you'll find and the easier it will be to access your humor resources when you need them the most.

11. I Had an Unhappy Childhood, So How Can I Laugh? Ever heard the expression, "It's never too late to have a happy childhood"? If you didn't have a happy childhood, or you're just coming out of an unhappy marriage or a horrible work situation, then all the more reason to start laughing now to make up for lost time. Laughter focuses us on the here-and-now, not on what happened 10 years ago or what might happen 2 years from tomorrow.

> *Life does not cease to be funny when people die any*
> *more than it ceases to be serious when people laugh.*
> — George Bernard Shaw

12. How Can I Laugh at a Time Like This? Gerald Coffee found laughter while captive as a prisoner of war. Viktor Frankl found humor in the midst of an internment camp. The person who put up a "More Open Than Usual" sign outside a bombed-out store in London found humor in the middle of World War II. The restaurant owner who posted the sign: "Waitress Wanted—Must Be Able to Swim" during a devastating flood found a reason to laugh. The Middle East hostages who nicknamed their morning church services "The Church of the Locked Door" found humor during a frightening ordeal. The Dumbbells, a Canadian comedy troop that performed for soldiers during World War I, found something to laugh about in the face of a tragic war. The speaker who put a "Handicapped" sticker on the back of his wheelchair so he wouldn't be towed away found humor in his life-altering predicament. And whoever had their tombstone engraved with "See, I Told You I Was Sick" found humor in the face of death.

Even with all these examples, and hundreds more like them, I'm still not sure I understand how people can laugh at "times like this." Sometimes I find it hard to laugh when I spill my Fruit Loops or when my favorite TV show didn't record properly. When I've asked people how they could *possibly* laugh during an unspeakable experience, their response is unsatisfying in its simplicity, yet overwhelmingly obvious. And the answer is always the same. "How could I *not* laugh?"

> *Humor counts most in precisely those situations*
> *where more decisive remedies fail.*
> — Berel Lang

• • • • • • • • • •

Those are just some of the humor blocks awaiting us. The great news is that all of them are removable. The reason we don't always laugh, even though we probably know humor can help, is that our sense of humor isn't just a pre-programmed channel we can automatically tap into. It is a skill and a discipline that we need to learn, use and practice.

Why Aren't You Laughing?

What a person finds funny says a lot about that person's background, beliefs, perceptions and overall psyche. What a person doesn't laugh at is just as revealing. Some psychologists believe that those areas that we feel are off limits to humor are the areas where many of our doubts, fears or uncertainties may lie.

*To laugh at what we hold sacred and still hold it
sacred is the highest form of humor.*
— Abraham Maslow

Is There a Worldwide Laughter Deficit?

A study reported at the International Congress on Humor, held in Basel, Switzerland, concluded that laughter is down two-thirds from what it was, worldwide, in the 1950s. People in the 50s laughed an average of 18 minutes a day; today, we laugh no more than 6 minutes a day. The researcher suggested this doesn't necessarily point to a decline in humor; it may, instead, be a by-product of our intermixing into more heterogeneous groups where political correctness and more restrictive social rules contribute to less open laughter in social situations. Other researchers have pointed out that our "laughter threshold" is much higher than it once was—it takes a lot more to make us laugh than it used to. So if you want to balance the old humor ledger of life—start laughing!

HUMOR-SQUASHING LANGUAGE

In chapter 6 we listed some examples of idea-busting language. There's a parallel here with *humor*-squashing language, most of which we heard growing up and some of which we still hear as adults.

Grow up!	How old are you?	Get serious!
Act your age.	You can't be serious!	Quit being silly!
Stay focused!	This is no time for fun.	What's so funny about this?
Are you insane?	Are you trying to be funny?	This isn't the time.
This isn't the place.	Don't you think this is important?	Let's get back to work.

Okay, Mike, put down the monkey and take that shower cap off your head right now!

The young man who has not wept is a savage and the old man who will not laugh a fool.
— George Santayana

DILBERT reprinted by permission of United Feature Syndicate, Inc.

ORGANIZATIONAL BLOCKS TO HUMOR

Laughter and good humor are the canaries in the mine of commerce – when the laughter dies, it's an early warning that life is ebbing from the enterprise.
— Paul Hawken

It's difficult enough getting past our inner voice that censors us when we think about being spontaneous and humorous. But then, once we *do* get past our own censors, we have this whole roomful of people, known affectionately as our co-workers, to worry about.

We've already mentioned several of the myths surrounding humor in the workplace in chapter 1. Organizations that promote a culture that fosters these myths—that the bottom line is more important than people, that humor has no business in a serious profession or that somehow humor will lead to anarchy—will obviously suppress humor at every turn. Here are some other organizational blocks.

1. Lack of Communication/Poor Morale. A communication vacuum fosters a climate of distrust, cynicism and rumors, which eventually leads to low morale. Although *subversive* humor thrives in organizations with low morale, *positive* humor, laughter and play suffer substantially. It's really quite simple: it's hard to have fun when no one's having fun. (I call this the "DUH" principle.)

2. "Keep Your Ideas to Yourself." As much as humor fuels creativity, the reverse is also true: creativity fosters a playful and humorous environment. Organizations that stifle creative contributions also suppress laughter.

3. "It's Nothing Personal." It's difficult to laugh in organizations that still don't realize that work *is* personal. Not only do successful organizations recognize this truism, but they also take care of the human being (employee, manager or customer) first and show concern for the entire person occupying a job, not just the person who shows up between nine and five. Some organizations now understand that if they help employees manage their entire lives, they end up with more motivated, fully functioning human beings. Human beings capable of laughing.

4. Autocratic Dictatorships. Authoritarian-style leaders tend to have a suppressed sense of humor and often stifle any sort of workplace fun. They are often perfectionists and are suspicious of other people who they see as a threat to their power. Autocrats also tend to use fear as a replacement for true leadership, and let's face it, as an employee, it's hard to laugh when you're afraid.

We lead by being human. We do not lead by being corporate, by being professional or by being institutional.
— Paul Hawken

5. "Let's Wait and See." Organizational cultures that encourage conservative, safe approaches to things and adopt a "let's wait for our competition to do it first" attitude tend to suppress risk taking and, as a direct result, end up discouraging humor in the workplace. Some people fear innovation and humor because they are not easily controlled. Both spring from our imagination, something that knows no rules or boundaries, and for some, that's a terrifying prospect.

6. Conformity Inc. If you enjoy playing "Where's Waldo?" then you'll enjoy this game. Look at a photograph of the board of directors of a large financial institution and see if you can find three differences between any of the over-50, white-haired, clean-shaven gentlemen wearing dark suit jackets with blue ties. It's challenging, isn't it? Many companies either overtly or unconsciously encourage conformity. The lesson for upcoming executives in these organizations is this: "If I act, dress, look and speak like the boss, I'll get promoted." In other words, leaders are selected not on their ability to lead, but on their ability to *follow*. And the values these organizations communicate to their staff is that conformity rules. Conformity is, after all, comfortable. The more we dress, think and speak alike, the more united we'll be, the more everyone will agree and, as a bonus, the easier it will be to spot "who's not on board." Funnily enough, many of these very same organizations often preach the need for creativity and boldness in the new economy.

Since humor often involves taking a step out of the zebra pack, and seeing things as white on black instead of as black on white, conformity can crush both humor and creativity. Conversely, the more we encourage people to be themselves and to bring their own personalities to the job, the easier it is to foster a climate of fun and enthusiasm.

> *If a company has two executives that think the same way, someone is redundant.*
> — Anon.

FINAL THOUGHTS

As with individual humor blocks, this has also been merely a jumping-off point for discussing organizational blocks. A myriad of other factors, including the physical environment, rewards system, level of stress, decision-making process, and employee recruiting, training and appraisal systems, have an impact on organizational culture. If we truly want to create energetic, exciting, creative and fun-filled workplaces where humor is a substantial part of the modus operandi, we need to focus on the overall culture and keep the interconnectedness of all these workplace elements firmly in mind.

Wow. That got a little heavy, didn't it? We need a joke, quick.

> *What did the fish say when it swam*
> *into the concrete barrier?*
> *Damn!*

And *that* is the final word on humor blocks, concrete or otherwise.

— 12 —

Practicing Safe Humor (How to Have Fun Without Getting Fired!)

Remember when your guidance counselor advised you that if you couldn't practice safe sex, you should keep it zipped? These prophetic words also ring true for the practice of safe humor, as in, "If you can't practice safe humor—keep it zipped (your mouth, that is)!"

Safe humor unites rather than divides people, focuses on solutions not problems, promotes creativity instead of squashing ideas and tears down walls instead of building barriers. Safe humor comes from the heart; unsafe humor comes from that imaginary devil guy sitting on your shoulder egging you on. Safe humor considers not only the content of the humor, but also the time, place, context and, above all else, the sensitivity and perspective of the audience, whether it's an audience of one or one thousand.

As everyone knows, humor is great medicine, but, as with any type of medicine, negative side effects can occur if it's administered incorrectly. This chapter provides a few precautions on how and when to administer humor most effectively without risking the health of the good-humor doctor or the patient.

When humor is meant to be taken seriously, it's no joke.

— Lionel Strachey, humorist

A TIME AND PLACE FOR HUMOR

The primary goal of this book is to encourage the use of humor in even the most serious situations and professions, so when it comes to defining parameters for what constitutes an inappropriate time and place for humor, the list is rather short. Given the power of humor and its overwhelming benefits, there are very few places where humor should be considered completely off limits. As we've seen, humor is a normal human reaction to dealing with a crisis, to solving problems and to coping with some of life's most difficult moments. Humor has helped holocaust survivors, hostage victims and prisoners of war survive. Humor helps people cope with terminal illness or overcome the death of a loved one. Humor therapy is used to treat mental health patients, assist people in overcoming drug and alcohol addictions and help new prisoners manage their loss of freedom. Given the tremendous impact humor can play in our lives, the *exclusion* of humor unequivocally does more harm than good. In fact, one of the first signs of a serious mental health problem is the *absence* of humor in a person's life. So if you still think there are places where humor is off limits, *please* re-read this book!

Okay, so there are a *few* work situations where we might want to tone down our sense of humor or at least be careful about *how* we use it.

1. Business travel through airport security. These folks, entrusted with ensuring our safety, are clearly hired for their lack of on-the-job humor. It's a criminal offense (included in the Aeronautics Act) to joke about carrying guns or a bomb aboard, so don't. (A former Tory housing minister had to resign his cabinet post after joking about having a gun at the Ottawa airport.) It's even dangerous to joke about poultry. When I travel with my assortment of humor props, I usually get searched and asked if I'm carrying poultry. The object of concern is the rubber chicken I travel with (my motto is: "never leave home without your rubber chicken"), and I've learned the hard way (can you say "strip-search"?) not to make any flippant remarks about turkey, chicken, or any form of poultry whatsoever.

2. Laying off staff. Although safe humor can soften the delivery of bad news, when it comes to firings or layoffs, it is best avoided. I know the temptation is to say something like, "Bob, you know how much you like golf? Well, I have some GREAT news for you . . ." This is not a good idea. Layoffs are the granddaddy of bad news in the workplace and must be handled as sensitively as possible. If the person on the receiving end of the news initiates some humor, then it may be okay to follow their lead, but keep the humor low key and, as always, from the heart.

DILBERT reprinted by permission of United Feature Syndicate, Inc.

3. International business. As more organizations enter the global business arena, the need to be sensitive about working with other nationalities and cultures increases. Different cultures have very different styles of humor, so the chances of offending someone are great if we start treading blindly into these uncharted humor seas. Even the *Foreign Service Journal Magazine* advises that "next to treason, making an inappropriate joke may rank as the 2nd most taboo practice in diplomacy."

In dealing with the Japanese, for example, anything that directs attention towards or embarrasses another person is considered taboo and not remotely funny. Japanese people will sometimes smile to mask their embarrassment, or even laugh in the face of tragic news as a way to minimize embarrassment for the deliverer of the news. And as a general rule, Japanese people will rarely smile for business photographs, no matter how casual or lighthearted the affair.

The Swiss have a very subtle, gentle approach to humor. Germans from the south of the country are known for their outgoing personalities and sense of humor, while Germans from the north are thought to be more serious. In Malaysia, people sometimes laugh to mask their anger. British humor often focuses on farce and slapstick. Even American and Canadian humor are different. Canadians tend to enjoy more sarcastic, satirical and self-effacing humor. (As a good Canadian, I should also mention that Canadian humor is substantially funnier than American humor). Besides being aware of the numerous cultural differences in humor and communication styles, we should be wary that a lot of humor stems from language, relying heavily on the use and understanding of a specific word or reference. Humor involving any sort of wordplay, including most jokes, does not translate easily across languages.

So when meeting and greeting and wining and dining in the international community, use humor sparingly and carefully. At the same time, remember that laughter knows no boundaries. If the opportunity for some safe humor arises, try it out. (I mean, the worst that can happen is you'll get deported or create an international incident. How bad could that be?)

4. Joking with the media. My only word of caution here is simply this: sometimes the media, in their quest for the perfect eight-second sound bite, will cut your interview off just before the part where you say, "I'm joking, of course!"

That's my exhaustive list of when to avoid humor. And even with these examples, it's not so much avoiding humor as simply considering the context of the situation and the content and style of humor being shared.

> *Damaging humor is often without insight. It is the cheap shot and insensitive. There is no challenge or real wit in it, no AHA! It leverages fear.*
> — Alexis Driscoll

Timing is Everything

An example of how context plays a role in the practice of safe humor occurred when a DILBERT cartoon, featuring a plane load of nuns crashing, ran in the newspapers in 1998. Now some might argue this topic is unsafe to begin with. What exacerbated its inappropriateness, however, was that purely by coincidence (the cartoons are drawn months in advance), it ran just days after the death of Mother Teresa. The timing and the context of world events resulted in many irate letters.

SAFE HUMOR WARNING:
THE FOLLOWING HUMOR IS RATED PG (POSITIVELY GREAT)

If we stick to our guidelines of safe humor as being sensitive to our audience and breaking down walls, then clearly it should be non-sexist, non-racist and non-discriminatory in content. The exceptions to this are when you watch a stand-up comedian of your choice or when you joke around with close friends and clearly know what each other's limits are.

Other workplace humor topics that are out of bounds include put-down humor directed towards your immediate family, humor about people's physical characteristics and, for bosses, any humor that highlights their position or power in the company. One final taboo topic is people's names. Joking about people's names is highly risky, because for many folks, "name jokes" were a major source of derision when they were growing up. Those memories of being bullied and razzed mercilessly on the school grounds are still too close to the surface for some.

Rule number one for practicing safe humor is know your audience. The filter to use when gauging humor safety isn't, "What do *I* find insensitive?" but rather, "What might my co-workers take exception to?" In fact, a 1993 U.S. Supreme Court decision in the U.S. changed a sexual harassment law regarding the use of sexual jokes to "what a reasonable *woman* would find offensive."

No matter how you deliver a joke, the folks around you may not know that you don't *really* believe all those things about "dumb blondes" or that your intent was well-meaning. And yes, I *do* think people worry way too much about being politically correct instead of being correct when it really matters, and yes, far too many people are uptight and need to lighten up a little (or maybe a lot). But, the reality is you are not going to help them lighten up by agitating them (trust me, I've agitated enough people in my time). We all have plenty of opportunities to be politically incorrect, sarcastic and insensitive when with our friends and loved ones; when it comes to the workplace, we need to be more accommodating to others' sensitivities. Now I know some of you are thinking, "But what is there left to laugh at?" Relax. Dozens of comedians, including Jerry Seinfeld, Jay Leno and Bob Newhart, have proven there are plenty of safe topics to laugh about if you keep your comic vision highly

Always practice *safe* humor.

(Cartoonist's footnote: No live animals were used in the drawing of this cartoon)

focused (and in the case of Seinfeld, ask "What's up with *that?*" a lot). And remember, jokes constitute only a tiny percentage of the humor spectrum, so there are umpteen ways to laugh without putting anyone down in the process. You might even look at practicing safe humor as a challenge—it's a great way to stretch your creative muscles and intellectual abilities.

If you do have a risqué joke that you can't resist telling, there are ways of making some jokes safer. For example, with ethnic jokes that could apply to *anyone*, remove the ethnic references and replace them with people from different towns, from your competition or your own profession. The joke then becomes: "What is the difference between a Torontonian and a Calgarian?" or "How can you identify someone who works for ACME Electronics?" WestJet Airlines provided an example of this on a flight when the attendant told the following joke over the intercom: "An airline attendant comes to a river and sees another attendant on the other side, so she asks the attendant how she can get to the other side. The attendant responds, 'You're already on the other side!'" Techniques like this rarely diminish the humorous impact, but still let you share your favorite one-liners. Changing the references softens the barbs, making them unlikely to be taken personally, even by the victims of the punchlines.

And finally, for proof that it truly is possible to practice clean humor, check out www.cleancomedians.com This is the web site of an organization known as Clean Comedians, which employs comics who deliver nothing but clean, wholesome and hilarious humor. They also have a two-volume book set available, *Comedy Comes Clean*, that further proves you don't need to get down and dirty to have a good laugh-fest. And if all that isn't enough, they even have a great acronym for filtering jokes: If a joke is G.R.O.S.S. (it's Gender-bashing, Racist, Obscene, Sexual in nature, or includes Swearing), it doesn't get used.

Wit has truth in it, wisecracking is merely calisthenics with words.

— Dorothy Parker

Humor Topics to Practice at Your Own Peril

Sex	Power/positional references
Religion	Families
People's names	People's physical traits
Ethnic/racial topics	Politics

MIRROR, MIRROR ON THE WALL—WHO'S THE FUNNIEST ONE OF ALL?

The safest form of humor is, well, you. Turning the punchline on yourself, laughing at your own mishaps and letting things roll off your back are all hallmarks of someone who truly has a great sense of humor. That's why blind comedians get away with jokes about being blind, or Jewish comedians jest about growing up Jewish.

Turning the punchline on yourself helps you overcome awkward or embarrassing situations with grace and humility and prevents other people from laughing *at* you, because you beat them to the punch every time. Laughing at yourself doesn't mean you're unsure

The 3 Golden Rules of Practicing Safe Humor

1. Laugh at yourself.

2. Laugh **with**, never **at**.

3. Find the humor in the **situation**, not the people.

about your abilities or lack confidence, to the contrary; it suggests you're confident enough to accept yourself, warts and all.

Prime Minister Jean Chrétien provided a textbook example of a leader who can laugh at himself (sometimes) during the spring of 1999. The Prime Minister was mugging for the cameras by shooting basketballs to demonstrate his tremendous vigor (in political speak: "Look at me voters, I'm shooting baskets therefore I'm good for at least another six federal elections") when he inadvertently did a face plant onto the pavement. The following day several Canadian newspapers ran cover photos of Chrétien down for the count sucking dirt. Although many people thought the papers crossed the line, Chrétien managed to rebound by grabbing the humor ball and running down court to score a few political points over the ensuing week by joking how the "people of Canada like to see their Prime Ministers down to earth" and how Nike was offering him a big endorsement contract.

> *You grow up the day you have the first real laugh at yourself.*
> — Ethel Barrymore

A word of caution though. Even when laughing at yourself, pick and choose the humor carefully. While it's great to laugh at your own everyday blunders, your early career mishaps or things you have no control over, like that receding hairline, be careful about using certain types of put-down humor on yourself. If, for example, you poke fun at your basic job skills or your ability to lead, people may start believing you and lose confidence in your capabilities ("Gee, maybe he really *doesn't* know what he's talking about?").

If you practice humor that parodies or picks on a certain department within your workplace, then make sure you are an "equal opportunity humorist." Picking lightheartedly on yourself, your own division or office, and *all* the other divisions lets you get away with more-barbed humor because people can see you are willing to turn the humor lens on yourself and paint everyone with an equal brush.

Finally, be careful about assuming that when someone *else* is laughing at his pot belly or her inept computing skills, this gives *you* free reign to join in the joking. Many people are comfortable laughing at themselves, but take offence at others poking fun at the same topic. I call this the old "it's-okay-if-*I*-pick-on-myself-just-don't-let-me-catch-*you*-picking-on-*me*" rule. (It's a long rule, but a good one.)

WARNING:
THE FOLLOWING HUMOR IS RATED "R" (RISKY)

NEVER BE SERIOUS SYNDROME

A potential, though rare, humor abuse in the workplace is overusing humor. If you respond to every situation with a comic's eye, you run the risk of not being taken seriously about anything. The safest way to have your humor accepted in the workplace is by making it clear, through your performance and your attitude, that you take your job seriously, just not yourself all the time.

CYBER-HUMOR—TO BOLDLY LAUGH WHERE NO ONE HAS LAUGHED BEFORE

A whole new world for budding jokers and humorists has opened up with e-mail and the internet. E-mail has dramatically changed the way we communicate. Instead of strolling over to a co-worker's desk, we now fire up our computer and launch a three-page missive. And sometimes we try to be funny. This is creating a whole new can of eels (you didn't know eels came in cans, did you?) under the heading of unsafe humor.

The challenge with cyber-humor is that written and verbal humor are two entirely different creatures. As many humorists have astutely observed, "the written word does not smile." Translation: subtle humor, sarcasm, ambiguity and irony are easily lost in e-mail messages because people don't have the benefit of face-to-face contact. Much of the effective delivery of humor rests in our facial expressions, body language and tone of voice. People can easily see your humorous intent by the twinkle in your eyes or a funny gesture. E-mail humor, however, can come across as flat or confusing, leaving the recipient with the burning question: "What the heck did she mean by *that?*"

Now don't get me wrong, I'm not saying we should ban humor in e-mail. Just be aware that certain forms of humor may not be as effective in cyberspace, and give some thought before hitting the send button. Also know that some companies are getting sensitive about employees forwarding each other obscene humor found on the internet. There has even been a few cases where an employee's computer has frozen up just as the boss walks in to discover the employee chuckling over lord knows what.

Both the *New York Times* and Xerox Corporation have fired employees for inappropriate internet use. Edward Jones & Company fired 19 people for forwarding pornography or off-color jokes. And e-mail messages, such as "25 Reasons Beer is Better Than Women," were submitted as evidence in a sexual-harassment claim at a subsidiary of Chevron Corporation. The claim was settled in 1995 for $2.2 million. (Now *that's* rich humor.)

Another form of cyber-humor to avoid is computer virus hoaxes. Many organizations and law enforcement agencies, including the RCMP's Information Technology Security Department, take computer virus or chain-letter jokes seriously. Their concern is that because so many hoaxes are lurking out there in cyberspace, people may ignore warnings about *real* computer viruses.

So practice safe cyber-humor kids. And if you can't, then place a giant condom over your computer and just say no!

CYBERSLACKING

With the advent of the internet and computer technology, there's a lot of debate about how much time employees spend surfing the web, downloading jokes or playing a few dozen rounds of solitaire to pass the time. A 2000 Angus Reid poll reported that Canadian workers waste 800 million hours a year surfing on the internet for personal reasons. These computer workplace pastimes are known as "cyberslacking."

To counter cyberslacking, some companies monitor computer use to ensure people are using their computers primarily for business purposes. But where is the line between wasteful cyberslacking and taking a much-needed regenerative break? If I'm advocating taking humor breaks, then what's wrong with spending 15 minutes on a computer game or searching for some good internet humor? Some psychologists, however, believe computer breaks aren't nearly as beneficial as other types of breaks. Many of us spend hours, or even most of our working days, tied to our computer, so playing a game on it doesn't provide the same mental break and change of stimulus needed during a stressful workday. Cyberslacking still involves staring at our monitors, sitting at our desks and using a tool that, for many, represents work. And as stress management experts suggest, even changing stressors is more beneficial than plodding ahead with the same type of activity.

Instead, we need to take breaks that engage our minds and bodies in a different activity and, ideally, connect us with other live humans. Studies of home-computer users suggest that people who spend even a moderate amount of time on their computer chatting in chat rooms and surfing the web waves tend to feel more depressed and lonelier. Computers are wonderful tools, but they are also socially isolating. If we truly want to tap into our human/humor resources, then we need to quit being mouse potatoes and make a concerted effort to turn off our computers and walk away from them for a while.

One final wacky thought on this subject (if you enjoy irony, you'll enjoy this). There are now internet addiction services available for folks who just can't pry themselves away from their computer. They're available on-line at a computer near you.

The Cost of Unsafe Humor

Unsafe humor divides teams, fosters distrust and cynicism, embarrasses both the originator and audience and, sometimes, gets you fired. Monica Traub, for example, was fired from her job as a trainee cook for the Royal Family after joking about how easy it would be to spike the Royal food. The Philippines' chief of staff was forced to resign after he joked with the media about the president's late-night drinking habits. A businessman in British Columbia was let go (a court later found him wrongfully dismissed) for sending lingerie to women in his office as a prank. And Canada's Avery Haines, a rookie news anchor, was fired after an "inappropriate" joke accidentally played on air.

ARE YOU BEING SARCASTIC?

Sarcasm, although beloved by many a stand-up comedian, should be avoided in the workplace whenever possible. Although most humor is stress-reducing, sarcasm is a form of humor that is potentially stress-*inducing*. Researchers have found that people who use heaping doses of sarcasm are more prone to heart attacks, presumably because of the negative emotional weight carried in sarcasm. Sarcasm comes from the Greek word sarkazo which means to "tear at flesh like a dog." So if you must use sarcasm, try tearing at your own hide instead of taking the chance of piercing someone else's sensitive rump.

> *Cynicism is humor in ill health.*
> — H.G. Wells

ISN'T IRONY IRONIC?

Irony is another dangerous form of humor in the workplace. Irony results when the intended meaning is the opposite of what is actually expressed. The use of irony in written correspondence or with new relationships often results in confused messages. As with sarcasm, irony is best left to the professional comedians who get paid to be ironic. Which seems rather ironic, now that I think about it.

> *There are very few good judges of humor, and they don't agree.*
> — Josh Billings

DANGER: REALLY UNSAFE HUMOR AHEAD

A word of caution for practical jokers. April Fool's Day is a great time to unleash your creative gremlins, but do keep this in mind: some victims of practical jokes have sued their tormentors, and even more unfortunate folks have died as a result of practical jokes gone awry. In Florida, some co-workers tossed a giant rubber snake into a construction hole and yelled "snake!" The poor man working in the pit died of a heart attack on the spot. In Louisiana, a fake kidnapping, intended as a practical joke, also resulted in the victim succumbing to a heart attack. And at a youth camp in Alberta, a worker dressed up in a bear costume to scare one of the Venture camp leaders, who had gone off to fetch some firewood. On the leader's return trip back through the dark forest, the fake bear leapt onto the trail and growled ferociously, startling the camp leader so badly that he threw the firewood. The costumed impostor was knocked unconscious by a flying piece of wood and had to be taken to the hospital.

These practical jokes gone haywire cast a whole new light on the term "safe humor." Practical jokes are a wonderful phenomenon, but ask yourself honestly how *you* would react being on the receiving end. And be prepared for a retaliatory attack, remembering what Mom always said, "It's all fun and games until someone loses an eye or dresses up in a bear costume and gets knocked unconscious."

> *Humor is laughter made from pain – not pain made from laughter.*
> — Dr. Joel Goodman, The Humor Project

Battle of the Comedians - Don Rickles vs. Bill Cosby

A 1970s research project looked at how often, and how loudly, different types of audiences laughed in response to different styles of humor. The study compared groups of strangers to groups of close friends and their responses to a friendly, low-key style of humor (as represented in this corner by Bill Cosby) versus a more caustic, sarcastic, unsafe style of humor (as represented in the other corner by Don Rickles).

The results were conclusive. Strangers laughed harder at the safe Cosby humor, but rarely laughed at Rickles, while close friends were more comfortable laughing at Don Rickles. This study reaffirms the need to consider the context of a situation and the audience when using humor. A gentler, low-key approach is the order of the day when working with new employees, when meeting representatives of another company for the first time or when working with a new client.

DILBERT reprinted by permission of United Feature Syndicate, Inc.

I'M JUST KIDDING!

There is a fine line between unacceptable, divisive humor and safe bantering, teasing or kidding around (honest, I'm not kidding about this). Industrial sociologists have observed that since the mid-1800s kidding in a work environment has been an important part of social bonding in team situations and is often used as a measure of acceptance. Although kidding or bantering can seem hostile or even cruel, the underlying subtext is always one of friendliness between the jokers. New employees, particularly men, use kidding as the ultimate measure of their acceptance as one of the gang. Think about the co-workers you'd never dream of kidding around with compared to those you spend a great deal of time cajoling. Chances are the ones you kid around with are thought to be more down to earth, approachable and likeable.

As Dacher Keltner, Ph.D., reported in the *Journal of Personality and Social Psychology*, teasing is an important social tool. While recognizing there is sometimes only a subtle difference between aggression and teasing, Keltner suggests that ultimately the driving force behind most teasing is to maintain good social relationships. Teasing helps form bonds, convey social standards and remove hierarchical boundaries by bringing everyone to the same level. Whether teasing is seen as safe or unsafe depends partly on the relationship between the teaser and the teased, and on the teaser's communication style. When people who are perceived as cold and aggressive tease other workers, the underlying intention is usually seen as hostile and is unwelcome. Keltner also notes that, in contrast to our own Western culture, many Central American and African societies are more comfortable with teasing as a daily form of communication. Some African-American children, for example, have developed a ritualized form of insulting each other, known as "sounding," as a tool for coping with hostility.

THE HUMOR DEFENSE

Humor can become a defensive shield to mask true emotions, avoid conflict or ignore valid criticism about work performance. It is sometimes easier to laugh things off than to deal with contentious issues head on. (This may be why comedians often come from troubled backgrounds, as they learned early on that humor is a powerful tool for deflecting conflicts.) Positive humor, however, is about using laughter to help us work through our problems, not hide from them behind a clown's mask. If you have co-workers or employees prone to this behavior, you may need to take them aside to make sure they are taking important messages seriously.

WHEN HUMOR GETS MESSY

Some groups use the vaudevillian "cream-pie-in-the-face" routine as a way to make political statements. The most famous of these groups, the Quebec-based Les Entartistes (which loosely translates as "the em-piers"), is dedicated to throwing pies at famous people who are deemed to take themselves too seriously. To date, victims of a walk-by "pie-ing" have included Microsoft's Bill Gates, actor Sylvester Stallone and even Canadian Prime Minister Jean Chrétien. Chrétien earned the distinction of being the first prime minister in history to be pied. His pier claimed to be part of the P.E.I. Pie Brigade, protesting for social reforms.

Defenders of the pie throwers say they are just practicing good, clean (but rather gooey) fun as a way to give a voice to people who feel powerless in the face of large corporations and uncaring politicians. Detractors claim it is, at best, a childish way to make a point, at worst, tantamount to physical assault.

In 1999, Les Entartistes pied federal Intergovernmental Affairs Minister Stephane Dion while he manned a lunch counter at a Montreal soup kitchen. Dion pursued legal charges. One year later, the two pie chuckers were convicted of dangerous assault and sentenced to six months probation and community service work. San Francisco Mayor William Brown also won his case against his pie-yielding attackers.

Attempting humor can be a sticky proposition.
Done right, you become an instant celebrity. Done
wrong, nobody wants to talk to you.
— Dick Camp

READING BETWEEN THE PUNCHLINES

The things that strike us as funny have the power
to set us free.
— Ron Jenkins, author of *Subversive Laughter*

Although subversive, unsafe humor should never be encouraged in the workplace, its presence can be advantageous. Why? Because for humor to be effective, there has to be some truth present. Of course, humor is silly and facts may get wildly exaggerated, but if there isn't at least a smidgen of truth in the humor, it is not effective. You should listen carefully, then, for the underlying truth spoken in subversive humor. If everyone is laughing about a certain issue, there's probably a good reason. If employees, for example, are continually exchanging *Dilbert* cartoons, it could be useful to see which topics are the most popular.

Subversive or cynical humor usually tries to diminish a powerful or unknown opponent. In a large organization, subversive humor can give power to employees who may feel powerless to effect any real change in the workplace. This style of humor is sometimes the *only* way that employees can level the hierarchical playing field in an organization.

Knowing there is an element of truth in all humor, you can use humor quite effectively to draw out the repressed feelings of employees. Many organizations, for example, hold skits during annual conferences or staff retreats, where employees act out different scenarios or play different members of the executive team. These are often events where people let their guard down and truly express what is on their minds. People feel more free to speak out through humor because of the context of the situation and the fact they are playing a part. These are perfect opportunities not just to laugh, but to open up communication channels and read between the humor lines to find out what the *real* workplace issues are.

In an interview in The Humor Project publication *Laughing Matters, Dilbert* creator Scott Adams describes a great example of how one organization is using subversive humor as a positive tool. The company has established a "Dilbertization Committee," whose function is to locate and eradicate any behavior that could end up being described in a Dilbert cartoon. (Incidentally, there's a wonderful verb now commonplace in many corporate offices. To be "Dilberted" is to be oppressed or exploited by a boss.)

In a similar vein, both the 1996 Bob Dole and Bill Clinton U.S. presidential campaign teams monitored the late-night talk shows to see what David Letterman and Jay Leno joked about when it came to their respective candidates. By monitoring the humor, they could tap into what issues were on voters' minds or see how certain statements were being interpreted. For example, Letterman joked: "A lot of people would look at a glass of water as half full, some as a glass half empty. Bob Dole looks at a glass and says, 'Man what a great place to put my dentures.'" For the Dole campaign team, jokes like this could signal the need to convince voters that his age was *not* a concern.

On a grander scale, subversive humor has given a voice to people throughout history who were powerless to express their ideas any other way. As early as 400 BC, Aristophanes, the first comedic playwright of note, scripted plays that dealt with sensitive public issues in a humorous light. Centuries later, comedians like Rick Mercer, from the television program *This Hour Has 22 Minutes*, has used humor to lampoon big banks as a way of deflating their power and providing a voice to people who feel powerless against corporate monoliths. More recently, Mercer initiated a "referendum" call – proposing that the Canadian Alliance leader's name, Stockwell Day, be officially changed to Doris Day, as a subversively humorous way of bringing attention to a controversial election campaign issue. And of course, editorial cartoonists often pen vicious cartoons aimed at exposing the follies of politicians.

Here are more examples (many of them are described in greater detail in Ron Jenkin's fascinating book *Subversive Laughter*) of how subversive humor has given a voice to people's concerns and leveled the playing field under some very oppressive situations.

🍂 In Charlie Chaplin's first talkie, the classic *The Great Dictator*, Chaplin plays dual roles as a persecuted, but spirited, ghetto barber and the hapless, egomaniacal dictator Adenoid Hynkle of Tomania. This 1940 film is a satire of Hitler and the rise of the Nazi regime. The film lampoons the Nazi party and paints Hynkle (Hitler) as a foolish, ignorant, vain and clumsy autocrat.

In one memorable scene, Hynkle prances around the room bouncing a giant globe as he dreams of world domination. Hynkle has assistants to lick his envelopes for him and at one point proudly proclaims, "Once the world is rid of Jews, then we can get rid of the brunettes." The film, while making us laugh, also reveals the utter stupidity and senselessness of the tragedy unfolding in Europe. By using subversive humor, Chaplin was able to psychologically diminish the power of Adolph Hitler. At the end of the film, Chaplin steps out of character and delivers an impassioned speech full of heart and anger, pleading to stop the madness. The speech was so powerful, Chaplin was asked to repeat it later on national radio. Subversive humor like this, working through our funny bone, helps us confront an issue we may otherwise not wish to see.

☂ Clowns in Bali regularly perform at state functions where the politicians take the clowns underlying messages seriously, which often poke fun at modernization and the ongoing threats of cultural and military invasions.

☂ During the Middle Ages traveling storytellers in Italy were known for their defiant comic spirit against social injustices.

☂ Clown-led rallies and parades demonstrated against apartheid in South Africa, while comedic theatrical plays helped to expose apartheid to the world.

☂ American slaves used humor and parody as a form of defiance.

☂ Prisoners of the Nazi occupation in Lithuania used humor to give them courage to fight for their freedom. Here, as in other situations, humor often replaced the need for actual physical violence.

Subversive humor, in short, can challenge our thinking, stir our emotions and diminish the authority of tyrannical figures. Subversive humor can sometimes cut to the heart of an issue with more finesse and power than any other form of communication. If, in oppressive regimes, subversive humor is the only voice people have to express their discontent and feel free, what does it say about workplaces where the dominant form of communication includes sarcasm, cynical jokes and politically subversive humor? What messages can be gleaned within the subversive humor in *your* workplace?

The very act of making fun of our inferior position raises us above it.

— Harvey Mindness

MANAGING UNSAFE HUMOR

Intelligence and a keen sense of what is right are at the heart of wit.

— Shelly Huston

Controlling inappropriate or unsafe humor is not easy. One person's inappropriate humor is another person's good clean fun. And you likely don't want to set up a "Joke Police Squad" and create the impression you are out to censor free speech. (Joseph Stalin actually jailed people who made political jokes, while Adolph Hitler set up joke courts to punish or even kill people who made fun of his government. This is probably not the best way to handle things in your workplace.) There are, however, a few simple solutions to consider.

1. Create a humor code of ethics. Write a simple set of guidelines (and for goodness sake, make it fun!) that lets everyone know you value humor in the workplace, but within certain limits. Spell out those limits as clearly as possible, explaining what type of humor is out of bounds. Include staff in the process so there is a greater chance of buy-in from everyone. You could even create a humorous video to illustrate the fun, wacky humor that is encouraged versus the unsafe humor that won't be tolerated.

2. Keep communication channels open. There tends to be a higher level of unsafe humor in workplaces where rumors abound and the level of trust is low. It's been shown, even with children, that honest and open communication diminishes the frequency of inappropriate humor.

3. Have unsafe jokers pay a fine into a coffee or social fund. In a group situation, use a simple majority-rules system to decide when a humorous reference crosses the line.

4. If you are on the receiving end of an offensive joke, consider the following:

🍸 If you're offended, start by asking yourself whether it's worth the effort to get upset or if, in the big scheme of things, it should just be laughed off. In other words, practice accessing your *own* sense of humor to put things in a proper perspective.

🍄 Don't laugh. If you didn't think it was funny, don't encourage more by pretending to laugh along with the crowd. Women are prone to do this in certain work situations to gain acceptance as "one of the guys." Children learn at an early age that if they re-route the humor and join in the laughter when someone else is being picked on, they will remain part of the gang and avoid becoming a target themselves. Some of that attitude carries over into adulthood.

🍄 Never respond with anger. If you get visibly upset, chances are that you, as opposed to the joker, will be labeled as having no sense of humor. Often this just increases the frequency of inappropriate jokes when someone realizes they can so easily "get a rise" out of you.

🍄 Never state the obvious, "That wasn't *funny*." This approach rarely works because the counterpoint is always "Yes, it was!" or "Can't take a joke, huh?" And in reality, even the most insensitive humor *will* be thought of as funny by some folks, so you can't win with this one.

🍄 Sometimes a simple "I don't get it?" or "Do you know any *funny* jokes?" will make people squirm, because the joker is forced to explain where the humor lies (usually in a pretty shallow place).

🍄 Offer to print the joke in an upcoming article you are writing for the company newsletter or to post it on the company web site. This often helps people see that their joke isn't appropriate for a wider (or perhaps *any*) audience.

🍄 Take the person aside afterwards and explain how "other people" may not have taken the joke the right way. This is a gentle approach that says to the joker, "I'm doing you a favor for future reference," instead of setting up a confrontational situation.

🍄 When appropriate, coach the person in how to give positive feedback rather than using sarcasm or point out that "If you included yourself in your joke, you'll get a better reception."

🍄 Focus on the issue, not the person. As with any conflict situation, if you label someone with a name like "you insensitive swine-hound," it will immediately escalate the situation.

🍄 Try using a "humor flip-flop" to flip the situation onto its back. Although there is a risk this could degenerate into a battle of wits (or halfwits), if done with finesse you might be able to turn around an awkward situation. Recall Churchill's humor flip-flop in chapter 3. Here's another of Churchill's classic humor responses. When invited to a new production of a George Bernard Shaw play, Shaw, in a written note to Churchill, asked him to bring along a friend, "if he has one." Churchill wrote back that he was unable to attend on the opening night of the play, but he would be happy to attend the second performance, "if there is one." Abraham Lincoln pulled a humor flip-flop when someone accused him of being two-faced. "If I had two faces," Lincoln replied, "would I use *this* one?"

A standard, all-purpose, humor flip-flop to use when you find the humor offensive might simply be, "You know, I have a great *sense* of humor, but right now I'm just not sensing any."

🍄 If a situation becomes a chronic problem and you cannot resolve it yourself, then, and only then, take it to a supervisor or manager.

Getting Work Back on Track

If too much fun threatens to take over the real work at hand, the leader of a group may need to gently nudge folks back on course. Humor *related* to a task tends to keep people focused on the here and now, whereas humor that strays tends to be more disruptive. Be careful, though, because in some cases an extended giggle-fest may be the very thing the productivity doctor ordered. Humor that detracts from productivity is only an issue if it becomes a chronic situation, in which case the leader or manager needs to look for the underlying reasons work is being derailed.

Laughing in the Face of Laughter

Each year, some unfortunate author is recipient of the British Literary Review Bad Sex Award. The award is given to honor the most pretentious, trite, overblown or embarrassing description of a sexual act written in a novel. The winner (or is that the loser?) is presented a small sculpture and asked to make an acceptance speech at a party. If the winner doesn't show up, he or she is threatened with the possibility of being replaced by a hired actor.

These sorts of awards, honors and tributes, designed to keep us humble, are out there in all shapes and sizes. When you are on the receiving end of a humorous-yet-rather-dubious honor or roast, you have two options. You can get angry, threaten legal action, or huff and puff until you prove to the world that you have an ego the size of the Grand Canyon and really can't take a joke. Or, as some authors who win the "Bad Sex Award" realize, the best antidote to the humiliation is to be a good sport and join in on the laughter. Phillip Hook, for example, winner of 1994's Bad Sex Award for a passage in *The Stonebreakers*, thanked the audience and the judges for some valid criticism, and then quipped that he was just going to have to do more research on the matter. He also joked that there must be a lot of competition in England for a bad sex award. His touchés and self-deprecating humor won the author many points with the crowd, who saw him as a humble, likeable and very human, human being.

> *He who has provoked the shaft of wit, cannot complain that he smarts from it.*
> — Samuel Johnson

CLOSING THOUGHTS

Don't let these cautionary words frighten you away from practicing humor. This chapter, like an airline attendant's talk about oxygen masks, is merely intended to guide you on those rare occasions when our humor engines fail us and we run the risk of nose diving into the muck. If you keep the words of humor author Allen Klein in mind, you won't go wrong practicing humor: "If our attempts at humor are gentle and from the heart, the risks are minimal; we cannot fail."

— *13* —

Guiding Lights for Adding Humor to the Workplace

To help light the humor path for you, here is a summary of guiding lights, some of which we've touched on throughout the book. Although some apply more to leaders and others need to be cast in a broader organizational context, all of them are relevant to the individual employee at any workplace. (Remember, as Lily Tomlin said, "We're all in this alone.")

① Be Sincere, Be Yourself

Courtney Page, one of the vibrant employees of Play, told me the key to having fun and being creative in their company is quite simple: "Everyone is allowed to be themselves. There is no line drawn between our work and personal lives. People are happier, more fun and more creative when they are free to be who they really are." And as comedian Jerry Seinfeld reminds us, "The whole object of comedy is to be yourself and the closer you get to that, the funnier you will be." So when practicing humor in the workplace don't try to be Robin Williams, just be yourself and be sincere. Do what comes naturally and *only* what is comfortable for you. If you try a style of humor that doesn't match your personality, chances are you'll feel awkward and it will show. Trying to force humor artificially into a situation is like trying to fit a square peg into a penguin—it really doesn't work and it gets very messy. Being sincere takes a *lot* less energy than playing any kind of forced role.

Southwest Airlines, even though it's known for hiring people with a well-developed sense of humor, stresses the need for its employees to be authentic. Airline attendants who are not naturally funny, aren't encouraged to be humorous over the public address system.

Being sincere means being true to your own voice ("authentic" comes from the Greek language, literally to "be your own author"), which means, on occasion, standing alone from the rest of the pack. So keep those immortal words of Yogi Berra close to your heart: "Don't always go where the crowd goes. It's too crowded."

> *There is a difference between acting funny and being funny. Don't act funny. Be human.*
> — Steve Smith, Director of Ringling Brothers &
> Barnum & Bailey Clown College

② Everyone Has Their Own Funny Bone

Don't assume that just because you think something is hysterical, everyone else will too. Our sense of humor is as unique as our fingerprints. One person's funny bone is another person's Achilles heel. So don't be disappointed if your humor falls flat or your co-workers aren't always on the same laughter frequency. In a survey conducted by *Psychology Today* magazine, more than 14,000 readers rated 30 jokes, and every joke was rated poor by some and great by others.

There are some general gender differences in our sense of humor. Men *tend* to be bigger fans of slapstick and low-brow humor (they're far more likely to appreciate *The Three Stooges*). Men also kid around more as a way of expressing affection. For some men, referring to their buddy's new haircut as a tragic boating accident is as close as they'll get to saying, "I love you big guy." In short, when adding humor to the workplace, respect and tolerate each other's differences.

In matters of humor, what is appealing to one per-
son is appalling to another.
— Melvin Helitzer

③ Look for Simple Ways to Add Humor

The wonderful thing about adding humor to work is that small gestures generate enormous payoffs. It's not, as a general rule, the expensive or grandiose changes that improve the quality of a workplace environment significantly. Surveys suggest that it's often just the small, simple things done *consistently* that dramatically improve workplace morale, like sending a simple hand-written card of thanks to someone or bringing in a box of donuts on Monday morning. Although big events are more memorable in our lives, it's the smaller, day-to-day things that have a major influence on our overall well-being. Another wonderful characteristic of humor is that it's highly contagious—it's easy to set in motion the domino effect with simply a dash of humor here or a sprinkle of laughter there.

It also pays to add humor slowly if you work in a conservative work environment. Don't try and overdo things or you'll run the risk of alienating folks. Like any other change in the workplace, even though we're talking about fun, you need to build support by getting management and staff onside, and then build momentum if you want to affect long-term changes to your organizational culture. Be sure to constantly celebrate the benefits of fun and humor in the workplace as a simple way to get more support.

The most wasted day of all is that in which we have
not laughed.
— Sebastian R.N. Chamfort

Spontaneity Rules!

One study found that 87% of the humor that occurred in a hospital was totally spontaneous. Spontaneous humor is often funnier than pre-planned humor, and it's the simplest way to add more fun into your workday.

---

④ Practice Safe Humor

This guiding light is so darned important I dedicated an entire chapter to it (you *have* read the book, haven't you?). To recap: practice positive, supportive humor that brings people together and tears down walls. Avoid sexist, racist or any other form of discriminatory humor. And learn to laugh at yourself.

> *The richest laugh is at no one's expense.*
> — Linda Loving

⑤ Don't Use Humor as Window Dressing

Humor shouldn't be viewed as a magical cure-all solution to more serious underlying workplace ailments. Long-standing issues must be resolved for any real changes to take place in your workplace culture. Humor can and, indeed, *should* be used to ferret out some of those issues, but if you use fun and humor merely to mask or ignore more serious problems, you'll do everyone a disservice.

> *If you can laugh at it, you can live with it.*
> — Erma Bombeck

⑥ Practice Looking for the Good

Look at the following math equations. What do you notice?

$$3 + 7 = 10$$
$$4 + 9 = 13$$
$$5 + 6 = 10$$
$$8 + 2 = 10$$
$$4 + 4 = 8$$
$$3 + 3 = 6$$

If you're like most people, you notice one equation is wrong. Like heat-seeking missiles, humans are programmed early on to find mistakes and spot the screw ups in life. Rather than seeing the five out of six that were right (83%!), like armchair coaches, we love pointing out the errors of everyone's ways and letting the whole world know, "YOU GOT ONE WRONG!" According to psychologists, 75% of our inner conversations with ourselves is negative talk. As trite as it sounds, we need to practice looking for the good in bad situations and in each other. Jack Canfield, co-author of the *Chicken Soup for the Soul* series, uses the term "inverse paranoids" to describe folks who believe other people are out to do them good. Let's face it, if you are constantly focused on what's not working, why something is a lousy idea or the top-10 reasons your co-worker is such a jerk, it's going to be that much harder to lighten up and find the humor in life's day-to-day situations.

Nothing erases unpleasant thoughts more quickly than concentration on pleasant ones.
— Hans Selye, stress researcher

7 Practice Fine Tuning Your Humor Vision

From there to here, from here to there, funny things are everywhere.
— Dr. Seuss

You *can* practice looking for humor in everyday life. Remember, funnier things don't happen to comedians, they just focus their comic vision on their daily lives to find the humor that's already out there waiting to be discovered. Humorists, comedians and comic writers have two things in common—they are curious and they are astute observers.

Have you noticed when you're thinking about buying a new car, you suddenly see that type of car *everywhere*? It's because your mind is tuned into that particular frequency— it's known as "selected perception." The same thing happens when you start looking for the humor in life. Suddenly things you may not have noticed before leap out wildly in front of your face.

Here are a few simple ways to fine-tune your humor sense.

- Read more humor—the comics, humorous novels and short stories. Listen to humor tapes on the drive home.

- Keep a humor journal. Write down funny thoughts, observations, anecdotes and jokes. This helps you remember them, forces you to think about them and lets you focus your comic vision without risk of embarrassment or failure. Make it a minimal goal to add one humorous item per week to a file or journal.

- Practice looking for the humor in bad situations. Take five minutes and ask yourself what's funny about a bad situation. Try the "things could be worse . . ." technique or practice reframing situations and looking at them from a comic writer's perspective.

- Vary your routine. Trying new things and changing the way you do everyday things is an easy prescription for nurturing creativity and your sense of humor.

- Practice being spontaneous until you get it right! It sounds like an oxymoron, but developing your sense of humor means letting go of some humor blocks and taking the risk of being spontaneous. And the great thing is you don't have to plan for it!

I tend to see the comical side of things - I call it seeing everything twice.

— Patrick McManus

I Found Some Humor!

During the early years of David Letterman's late-night talk show, much of the humor was known as "found humor." The producers would send Dave out with a camera into regular, everyday situations, and he would literally "find" the humor—on a trip to the shoe store, riding an elevator or driving through the pick-up window at a fast-food restaurant.

⑧ Put People First

Humor is a distinctly human trait, so putting humor to work means recognizing that to be successful in any line of work, you have to put people first, whether those people are your clients, patients, superiors, co-workers or employees. In a world of bottom lines, profits and technology, touching each other through laughter is about valuing human connections and relationships. Being human first, and a businessperson second, *is* good business. And when you truly practice putting people first, humor will follow naturally.

> *If you wish to glimpse inside a human soul and get to know someone, just watch them laugh. If they laugh well they are a good person.*
> — Fyodor Dostoevski

⑨ Learn to Love Bloopers

Remember the old 50-50-90 rule: "Anytime there's a 50% chance of getting something right, there's a 90% chance you'll get it wrong." Learning to love your bloopers is a common theme throughout this book because it's one of the easiest ways to start laughing more often. A perfectionist attitude is a recipe for leading an overly somber and serious life. Conversely, laughing at our fumbles, besides being a reliable way to cope with stress, keeps us humble. As well, laughing at our bloopers fosters a climate of creativity by encouraging people to take risks without fear of embarrassment. So forgive yourself, forgive others and laugh more often.

> *When we admit our schnozzles instead of defending them, we begin to laugh and the world laughs with us.*
> — Jimmy Durante

Oops!

Among the dozens of humor files I collect is one dedicated strictly to celebrating life's blunders and bloopers. It reminds me that looking for bloopers is one of the easiest ways to find and add more humor to my life. Bloopers are everywhere. Within my ever-expanding blooper file, I've amassed newspaper headline bloopers, insurance report blunders, court transcript quotes, famous celebrity misquotes, school paper blunders, sign bloopers, translated ad blunders, church bulletin board misquotes, stupid criminal stories, job interview bloopers, label instruction blunders, manager misquotes, and a whole raft of miscellaneous odds and sods that can only fit under the nebulous heading of "oops" (like the story about an airplane that was delayed because the pilot had a fear of flying or the tale of a fellow who found his missing cell phone after it rang inside his dog's stomach).

So be on the hunt for bloopers, including your own, and start your own "oops" file. It's a simple way to remind yourself that we all make mistakes. Here are a few morsels from my files.

Newspaper headlines:	Larger Kangaroos Leap Farther Study Finds Sex, Pregnancy Link Lack of Brains Hinders Research
Church bulletin board:	Don't Let Worry Kill You – Let the Church Help This being Easter Sunday, we ask Mrs. Lewis to come forward and lay an egg on the altar.
Lawyer transcripts:	"How many times have you committed suicide?" "Was it you, or your younger brother, who was killed in the war?"
Insurance report:	"The guy was all over the road. I had to swerve several times before I hit him."
Silly tourist questions:	"At what elevation does an elk become a moose?" "That's a lovely Canadian flag you have – does it come in other colors?" "Is it true that to escape a bear you have to climb a tree that's the same width as your head?"

⑩ Practice Relevant Humor

Just as every profession has its own unique jargon, it also has its own brand of humor. Humor is most effective when it speaks to something everyone can relate to. For that reason, relevant humor that connects to your profession, organization or office will have the most resonance. Not only is relevant humor funnier, it also helps to create a sense of shared history by becoming part of an organization's personality and distinctive tenor.

Here's some suggestions for practicing relevant humor.

- ☂ Start an office humor file where everyone can submit funny work-related jokes, stories, photographs, bloopers or articles.

- ☂ Create a humor bulletin board specifically for workplace humor.

- ☂ Start an office humor journal that anyone can add humorous workplace experiences to.

- ☂ Scan and clip humorous articles or stories from association newsletters and trade magazines.

- ☂ Search the web. There's humor for every profession out there somewhere on the web.

- ☂ Have a regular humor column in your newsletter, web site or annual report to celebrate your humor.

There is no joy in living without joy in work.
— Thomas Aquinas

⑪ Blend in the Humor

Look for opportunities to blend fun and humor into existing workplace practices. Don't just treat it as something you switch off and on. The more integrated the humor becomes, the more successful you'll be at achieving a productive balance between work and play.

My definition of self-actualization is when you are
confused about the difference between work and play.
— Ken Blanchard

⑫ Hire for Humor

If you want to add more fun to your work environment, then bring people into your organization who are energetic, passionate and have a well-developed sense of humor. Some managers have suggested that this may be the most important thing you can do to create a fun-filled work atmosphere. Assessing potential candidates' emotional intelligence and their ability to be creative, to problem solve, to manage stress and to interact with other live human beings has never been more important. Unfortunately, traditional interview processes often fail to select the right people in today's work climate.

Start by including a good sense of humor as one of the core components of any job description. Then consider taking an offbeat approach to finding potential job candidates, as a way of sending the message that you are looking for creative and fun people. The web site recruiting page for Ben and Jerry's Ice Cream, for example, has a goofy picture of Ben and Jerry wearing large ice cream bucket-like hats with the caption "We Want You!" Southwest Airlines has used recruitment ads with a picture of CEO Herb Kelleher wearing an Elvis Presley-style jumpsuit, with the caption, "Work in a place where Elvis has been spotted."

Now admittedly, evaluating someone's sense of humor is a tricky undertaking, but there are some simple ways you can at least get a sense of someone's humor sense. Reference checks can determine if candidates contributed to a positive team atmosphere at their previous employment. Situational questions can determine how candidates might use humor to manage stress in a pressure situation. Ask them how they would contribute to a positive and fun work atmosphere and what they think the role of a good sense of humor is in a work situation. Or get a little more creative.

At Amy's Ice Cream, a chain based in Austin, Texas, potential candidates must pass the "paper bag test." Each prospective employee is given a white paper bag and told to be creative. The results have been everything from paper masks to bags containing homemade videos. At Trilogy Software, the hiring supervisors are known to take candidates rollerblading or out on some other fun activity as part of the post-interview selection process. And at Netscape, engineers have been handed Silly Putty as part of their interview process.

Even NASA has suggested they need to hire astronauts with

a good sense of humor. JoAnna Wood, the supervisor of psychology and behavior laboratory at the Johnson Space Center, spent a few years studying scientific teams in Antarctica and found that rising tensions were the number one problem. As reported in an article for the Associated Press, according to Wood, the three most important traits needed in long-term work situations (which future astronauts may find themselves in) are emotional maturity, flexibility and a sense of humor.

> *I want to see an ad . . .Wanted: nonconformist, dissenter and rebel; must also be able to add.*
> — Tom Peters

⑬ Add Humor to Your List of Values, Mission or Vision Statement

The human resources consulting firm William M. Mercer reported that 8% of 286 employers surveyed have a written mission or goal that included the need to incorporate humor or fun into their day-to-day work. Yet, almost everyone I've questioned has told me they believe humor is important and that, ideally, they would like to have more fun on their job. If it's important for your organization to have a people-centered, fun environment, then back it up by saying so in your mission statement and list of core values.

The corporate motto for Grimes Aerospace in Columbus, Ohio, for example, is "Growth, Profit and Fun." At Play, their three-word mission is: People * Play * Profit. Play also posts the company's six values (open-mindedness, passion, respect, energy, enrichment and support) on their office walls. And Tim Monaghan, founder of Domino's Pizza, lists "Have Fun" as one of the key ways to build a successful company.

If you value humor, say so!

> *Purpose and laughter are the twins that must not separate.*
> — Robert K. Greenleaf

⑭ Offer Humor in the Workplace Training

Once you've listed humor as one of your core values and included it in your mission statement, back it up by offering staff training in humor in the workplace, creativity, and stress management. At the very least, create a humor resources library, complete with training cassettes, videos and books.

The human race has only one truly effective weapon and that is laughter.
— Mark Twain

15 Plan to Have Fun

If you are serious about humor, then treat it like any other workplace priority and plan for it. Some overburdened executives have told me that the only way they achieved balance in their life was by setting specific, measurable targets (for example, committing to being home for family meals at least 20 times per month). What works for stressed-out executives works for stressed-out organizations. So include fun activities and specific humor goals as part of your work plans, goals and targets.

People rarely succeed unless they have fun in what they are doing.
— Dale Carnegie

16 Encourage Leadership With Laughter

As we've seen throughout this book, humor helps leaders build rapport and trust with employees, manage creativity, promote open communication and motivate employees to new levels of performance. In fact, according to Israeli psychologist Avner Ziv, a person's sense of humor may be a better predictor of leadership abilities than their IQ level. It makes sense, then, that many leaders are leading with laughter.

Like orchestra conductors, leaders set the tone for an entire company through their actions and attitude. As a leader, laughing at yourself and your own blunders encourages employees to admit their own mistakes without fear of recrimination and keeps you humble. A report by the Forum Corporation suggested that practicing humility is a key way to build trust with employees or co-workers. When managers admitted their mistakes, they were felt to be *more* competent, not less.

Many successful leaders are known for their abundant sense of humor. Sam Walton, the late former president of Wal-Mart, challenged his employees to exceed a quota for earnings projections, promising that if they did, he would wear a hula skirt and dance down Wall Street. They exceeded the target and Walton danced. The CEO of Great Plains Software publicly smashed three eggs over his head as he explained three big mistakes he had made in the previous year.

Leaders, however, must be especially careful about practicing safe humor. Managers should avoid humor that plays on their position or power in any manner. Instead, practice positive humor that strengthens teamwork, builds confidence and rewards accomplishments.

> *A leader without a sense of humor is like a lawn mower at the cemetery – they have lots of people under them, but nobody is paying them any attention.*
> — Bob Ross

17 Keep the Humor Spirit Alive

Adding humor into a workplace isn't a 1, 2 or even 10 times a year event. It's an ongoing, day-to-day attitude that permeates every level of an organization.

To give humor a boost in your workplace, create a "Humor Squad" of dedicated, enthusiastic folks to help keep your humor spirit alive. Southwest Airlines, for example, has a culture committee that helps promote the vision and values of the organization.

> *Remember that happiness is a way of travel – not a destination.*
> — Roy M. Goodman

18 Evaluate and Reward Your Sense of Humor

We tend to value what we can measure, so on a regular basis, ask yourself, "Are we having fun yet?" On at least a yearly basis, have some way of tracking your company's success in terms of its level of fun, motivation and commitment by employees and customers. And reward employees or departments who show a commitment to workplace spirit and humor.

> *He who laughs, lasts!*
> — Mary Pettibone Poole

PARTING THOUGHTS - GIVE YOURSELF PERMISSION TO PLAY

Each autumn, polar bears congregate near Churchill, Manitoba, waiting for the ice to form on Hudson Bay so they can head north to their winter feeding grounds. Often these polar bears wander into the town of Churchill. On one particular occasion, a bear roamed onto the grounds of a local dog sled team. Ordinarily, this would be cause for concern, as these bears have gone months without food and wouldn't necessarily pass up the chance for some fresh dog meat. Instead of a violent confrontation between the bear and dogs, though, these furry four-legged carnivores began playing with one another. Why? Likely because the dogs invited the bear to play. By getting down into the lowered-head, tail-wagging, bum-in-the-air-position, the dogs sent the message to the bear that play would be welcome. Which is exactly what these unlikely playmates did.

So take a lesson from these dogs and invite people and customers to play at work, simply by giving them permission to do so. For new employees, this might mean handing out a "Humor Guide" to your organization or sending them on a fun scavenger hunt as part of their orientation. At Insystems Technology Inc., employees receive a watch and a jar of candy on their first day.

The Longaberger Company, which makes handcrafted items in Ohio, insists that all employees spend at least one-quarter of their 35-hour work week having fun. David Dauffield, CEO of computer software company PeopleSoft, encourages new employees to have fun when he welcomes them, telling them bluntly that if they're not having fun, they should quit.

This last guiding light is the most important one. I truly believe everyone still has that five-year-old buried inside them, and what most people are waiting for is simply permission to have fun and laugh. When I work with senior executives in humor and stress-management workshops, I am continually amazed by the transformation in people as they change from somber, serious and, in some cases, harried-looking "professionals" to a group of creative, playful and imaginative human beings. How do I achieve this seemingly magical transformation? Simply by creating a safe environment, setting the tone by example, gaining their trust, moving slowly and, above all else, giving them *permission* to be a little silly, to laugh, to screw up and to be themselves. Once you've given yourself and each other permission to have fun, the rest is child's play.

> *To laugh and love much . . . to leave the world a bit better . . . to have played and laughed with enthusiasm and sung with exaltation . . . that is to have succeeded.*

— Ralph Waldo Emerson

"With these new glasses I can see humor everywhere!"

— 14 —

201 Ways to Put Humor and Fun to Work

Not all of these suggestions will be relevant or appropriate for your particular profession or workplace, but hopefully, out of this summary checklist of ideas, you'll find a few ideas, or at least seeds of ideas, for your particular situation.

STRESS BUSTING WITH HUMOR

Reframe Your Stressor

1. Take five minutes to write down "what's working," "what's positive" and "what's remotely funny" about an issue causing you stress.
2. Imagine the worst-case scenario. Exaggerate and have fun with the wildest possibilities to gain a more balanced view of a problem.
3. Imagine a positive reference point for you—last summer at the cabin, last weekend at the ski hill—anything that allows your mind to travel to a positive place.

4. Create your own silly version of a "Top-10 Ways to Deal With Stress" list and then read it to yourself the next time you're feeling stressed out.
5. Have a slogan or goofy song to recall every time you face a stressful situation.
6. Reframe the event by looking at it through the eyes of your favorite comedian or superhero.
7. Ask yourself . . . what's the *one* thing from this mess that I can take away, learn from or laugh at?
8. Imagine a wacky newspaper headline describing the event.
9. Complete the following sentence, "It could be worse . . . "
10. Switch sides in a debate and argue to ridiculous extremes from the other side.
11. Count to 10 and imagine how funny it will seem a year from today.
12. Visualize people you're mad at as the name you'd like to call them.
13. Come up with a funny label or code to describe your common stressors.

Reward Yourself
14. Make a list of three simple and fun rewards to give yourself whenever you have to deal with a recurring workplace stressor.
15. Create an "I'm Having a Bad Day" prize and have it ready to give to someone who *really* needs it.

Relax
16. Make a silly face.
17. Start smiling. Even fake smiling produces some of the same benefits as a real smile.
18. Start to laugh. Even fake laughing can produce some of the same positive physiological benefits as real laughing.
19. Create a humor first aid kit full of cartoon books, funny videos, pictures or zany props—anything that allows you to access your sense of humor as quickly as possible.
20. Take a humor break—read a joke book, watch 10 minutes of a funny video or juggle.
21. Find someone outside your workplace to talk and laugh with.
22. Find a "Stress Buster" partner in the workplace, someone who you can call the next time you feel tempted to push the photocopier out the window.

23. Have a goofy hat or clothing item you can put on every time you feel stressed, or wear something wacky under your business clothes to remind you to keep cool when the heat is on.
24. Find the nearest four-year-old—kids can do wonders for your nerves. (*Caution: If a kid is causing you stress, find the nearest 40-year-old.*)
25. Create an "end-of-the-workday" ritual to leave work behind (write down outstanding issues and lock them away, play a goofy song or put on a clown nose).
26. Create a weekends/time-off only calendar so that you don't bring work issues home with you.

Relax by Lightening Up Your Office

27. Work to music – some studies show it helps productivity and creativity.
28. Allow staff to personalize their work areas in fun ways.
29. Program your computers to play inspirational music each time they start.
30. Create fun computer screen savers.
31. Create an official "Lighten Up!" room with books, posters, videos and toys.
32. Decorate your office with humorous posters, pictures and props.
33. Create a humor bulletin board.
34. Create your own "hall of fame" photo gallery, highlighting employees and achievements.
35. Create a giant-sized mascot for display in your office.
36. Post a humorous quote or thought of the day somewhere highly visible.

HUMOR ON THE ROAD— LAUGHING DURING THE COMMUTE

37. Hang a "Lighten Up!" reminder symbol from your rear-view mirror.
38. Put humorous signs or buttons on the dashboard.
39. Keep a funny stress-relieving prop handy in the glove compartment.
40. Create a technology-free zone in the car. Turn your cell phone and computer off!
41. Listen to comedy tapes or CDs.
42. Sing along to the radio.
43. Make up silly songs as you drive.

44. Search for humorous bumper stickers.
45. Reframe annoying drivers by imagining them as the insult you want to hurl at them.
46. Start silly traditions in your car pool like rewarding whoever arrives with the best joke.

MANAGING CHANGE THROUGH HUMOR

47. Create a humorous newsletter or video to introduce the change.
48. Develop a wacky "Top-10 Reasons to Change" checklist.
49. Design a talk show or "town hall" format to get employee input.
50. Humorously reframe the change by developing a list of "The goods news about the change is . . ., the bad news is . . ."
51. Create a quiz-style game show to help teach people about the changes going on.
52. Create a fun slogan to promote the change and post it everywhere.
53. Hold a fun "Whine and Cheese" party to give employees a chance to express their concerns in a non-threatening forum.
54. Poke fun at harmless blunders and setbacks along the way.
55. Create fun contests to encourage employees to get involved.
56. Create a wacky automated phone system to record people's opinions about the change.
57. Reward employees and departments for embracing the change.

HUMOR AS A CREATIVITY CATALYST

58. Hold regular brainstorming sessions.
59. Brainstorm a humorous topic or play improv games before settling down to brainstorm the more serious topic at hand.
60. Brainstorm in a fun location like a park, a museum or the zoo.
61. Use fun distractions like toys, wacky props or costume items to encourage creative thinking during brainstorms.
62. Brainstorm a list of idea-busting phrases.
63. Create fun penalties for people who use idea-busting language.
64. Brainstorm the opposite of a problem to force a different perspective.
65. Look at the problem or issue from a different profession's perspective.
66. Make random associations with the issue to force a changed perspective.

MOTIVATING THE TROOPS

And the Winner is . . . Rewarding and Saying Thanks

67. Hold a fun awards ceremony midway through a particularly stressful period to give people a break and an energizer.
68. Create awards that encourage appropriate behavior.
69. Create some just-plain-silly awards.
70. Create fun *team* awards to promote teamwork and friendly competition between teams.
71. Imitate the Oscars or Emmys when presenting the awards.
72. Hold contests that involve all employees or even their families, for example, hold a contest for a new company jingle, motto or slogan.
73. Have a "welcome to the company" party for new employees (instead of just "sorry you're leaving the company" parties).
74. Develop a list of possible rewards that employees can receive— be creative.
75. Show appreciation to spouses and/or family members when employees are putting in long hours or traveling on business— say thanks with a card, movie tickets or flowers.
76. Have a "pass-the-thanks" day when one bouquet of flowers or box of chocolates is passed at regular intervals from desk to desk (accompanied with a reason the person is passing it on).
77. Tape small treats, like Hershey Kisses, to memos.
78. Deliver a rousing standing ovation for everyone who makes it to work on a Monday morning.
79. Stockpile a supply of humorous thank you cards to make thanking people easy.
80. Give away a free lunch a day or a week in the staff cafeteria.
81. Hold a contest for the best team name or slogan.
82. Celebrate every small victory.

Getting to Know You

83. Hold social events on a *regular* basis—they *don't* have to be elaborate or expensive.
84. Have lunch/breakfast/dinner at a different staff member's house every two months.
85. Keep an office calendar with significant dates, birthdays, milestones, etc.
86. Create a customized office calendar with employee photos.
87. Hold team sporting events—darts, baseball, bowling, anything that gets everyone involved.

88. Hold your own Olympics with events relevant to your profession.
89. Hold job-swap days to encourage staff to experience each other's workday.
90. Hold a family open house where family members can tour the office and meet co-workers.
91. Keep a fun photo album or scrapbook for staff and clients to view.
92. Hold a "match the employee to the baby picture" contest.
93. Hold a "match the employee to the attribute" contest (e.g., favorite movie, sport or animal).
94. Hold a "match the employee to their pet" contest.
95. Hold an employee scavenger hunt—give people a week to find other staff members who match a list of attributes.
96. Personalize those dry organization charts by scanning in photos of the actual people, of their baby pictures and/or listing some personal qualities related to each person.
97. Keep lists of people's "isms"—common sayings, flubs, or favorite words that have become a trademark for that particular person.
98. E-mail out a "Meet _____," featuring a new employee every week, and including a fun picture and some fun personal information.
99. Grab the whole team and meet someone at the airport the next time they return from a business trip.
100. Compile a list of staff names as they appear on the computer spell checker and create an alternate employee phone list with their new nicknames.
101. Invite retirees and former employees to social functions.

Miscellaneous Motivators

102. Create campaign-style buttons for staff to wear to remind people to lighten up!
103. Assign secret buddies to perform unexpected acts of fun for their secret partner.
104. Create a fun company song, slogan or cheer.
105. Create a fun company mascot.
106. Create a fun start-of-the-workday (or week) ritual.
107. Create a fun end-of-the-workday (or week) ritual.
108. Get involved in a fun community charity program.
109. Create a giant wall mural where employees can add thoughts, ideas, or quotes.
110. Keep a journal or book of successes.
111. Create a humor section on your web site or company newsletter.

112. Hold a weekly or monthly employee slide or home video show during a lunch hour.
113. Hold a staff picnic in the dead of winter.
114. Add cartoons and humorous quotes to inter-office memos.
115. Create a dictionary of terms only your company would use or understand.
116. Create fake alternative business cards to describe the real person with a more creative, imaginary title that *really* captures their true spirit and job description.
117. Create a fake membership I.D. card for your professional association.
118. Have a warm, funny office door sign that lets people know you're a warm, funny, caring, approachable, lovable kind of person.
119. Create a humor file or journal of jokes, quotes and anecdotes relevant to your particular profession.
120. Form a Fun Squad or Stress Busters Department.
121. Have theme days (or weeks or months).
122. Give yourself a nickname based on your spell-check name or the last four digits of your work phone number (for example, if your extension is 3764, you could be "Frog").
123. Hold an office scavenger hunt.
124. Hold an office Easter egg hunt.
125. Create an annual yearbook of your company's highlights, complete with fun photos, memorable moments, significant dates, employee profiles, etc.

CUSTOMER SERVICE WITH SOME LAUGHTER

126. Add a humorous caption, quote or image to your business cards.
127. Look for opportunities to add some humor to all your advertising.
128. Add some humor to signs.
129. Create a humorous service slogan.
130. Add some humor to your voice mail system.
131. Create a fun waiting room or reception area.
132. Add some humor to any instructions or regulations designed for customers.
133. Include customers in theme events or company celebrations.
134. Say thanks to customers in a creative way.
135. Devise some humorous contests for customers.
136. Add a humorous quote or cartoon to invoices, bills or receipts.

MEETINGS FOR THE SERIOUSLY CHALLENGED

137. Create agendas with catchy titles, cartoons, jokes or quotes.
138. Have a theme agenda (e.g., use movie titles to describe agenda items).
139. Include a humor break in every agenda.
140. Name your meeting room or boardroom something fun and inspiring.
141. Hold meetings at your house, a local picnic site, a park or the bowling alley—anywhere that breaks people out of the routine and creates a relaxed atmosphere.
142. Lighten up and liven up your meeting room with fun props and posters.
143. Have door prizes at every meeting.
144. Have a fun penalty for late arrivals.
145. Start each meeting with a fun tradition.
146. Create fun penalties for ramblers or people who stray from the agenda topic.
147. Add a rumor mill section at the end of every meeting.
148. Have a "whine and cheese" section in the agenda where people are allowed two minutes to vent and whine in an exaggerated, over-dramatic manner.
149. Have awards for the best work-related funny story, joke or blooper for each meeting.
150. Try holding meetings without chairs for faster meetings with a totally different perspective.
151. Play "jargon bingo" during meetings (make bingo cards featuring overused phrases and words related to your profession) as a way to reduce babble speak.
152. Have a "pick your nose" meeting, where everyone has to don a clown nose, animal nose or Groucho Marx nose.
153. Have an official bonehead or foot-in-mouth award each time someone makes an inappropriate comment.
154. Create an official Meeting Jester position for each meeting.
155. Bring fun food and match it to the theme of the meeting.
156. End meetings with a fun, upbeat, work-related anecdote or game to leave people feeling positive and energized.

SPEAKING OF HUMOR

157. Laugh at your own flubs throughout your talk.

158. Create a list of standard humorous recovery lines for when bloopers occur.
159. Tell amusing anecdotes that deliver a message.
160. Use jokes that are current, safe, relevant to your topic and deliver a message.
161. Create a humorous introduction for yourself.
162. Find out any audience "in" jokes beforehand.
163. Use wacky props to illustrate a point.
164. Use a fun video clip.
165. Add some fun sound effects.
166. Intersperse humorous overheads (e.g., one of the family dog) with the serious ones.
167. Add cartoons or humorous quotes to overheads or slides.
168. Exaggerate a point to find some humor.
169. Marry unrelated ideas.
170. Look at your topic from the opposite perspective.
171. Parody a famous book, movie or television show.
172. Use the Rule of Threes or the bait-and-switch routine to set up a humorous list.
173. Use humorous quotes related to your topic.
174. Use interesting or amusing trivia or statistics to make a point.
175. Create a funny top-10 list related to the topic.
176. Create a "what's in and what's out" list.
177. Create a "The Goods News is . . . and the Bad News is . . ." set up.
178. Throw fun things out into the audience.
179. Use excessive repetition to generate some laughs.
180. Incorporate funny surveys or survey the audience about something fun.
181. Add humor to handouts.
182. Use participants' names on all handouts.
183. Look for funny or unusual industry terms or acronyms to have fun with.
184. Poke fun at the boss (with her permission).
185. Plant amusing questions in the audience.
186. Incorporate some magic tricks.
187. Find some humor in a "This Day in History" reference.
188. Role play using audience volunteers.
189. Create a game show-style quiz.
190. Hand out fun door prizes.
191. Incorporate wordplay.
192. Come with a fun group name for your audience (e.g., a flight of airline pilots).

Putting Humor to Work

193. Look for some humor in the location of the event.
194. Look for humor in the weather.

KEEPING THE HUMOR SPIRIT ALIVE

195. Hire employees who have a well developed sense of humor.
196. Include fun or humor in your organization's mission statement and list of values.
197. Create a "Humor Code of Conduct."
198. Offer periodic training in humor and creativity in the workplace.
199. Create a humor and creativity library of books and tapes.
200. Include fun activities in work plans – make fun a priority!
201. Evaluate your organization's sense of humor – are you having fun yet?

— APPENDIX —

Tapping into Some Humor Resources

Speaking of Ideas

Keynote talks and workshops on various aspects of humor in the workplace are offered, including: You Can't Be Serious! Put Humor to Work; Humor as a Stress Buster; and Managing to Have Fun – Humor Skills for Leaders.

> Contact: Michael Kerr, 322 Canyon Close, Canmore, Alberta
> T1W 1H4
> 1 (866) 609-2640, mkerr@banff.net, www.mikekerr.com

The Humor Project

The Humor Project is based in Saratoga Springs, New York. It includes a humor catalog full of humor resources, a speakers' bureau and two annual conferences dealing with humor.

> For information, contact: 480 Broadway, Suite 210,
> Saratoga Springs, New York 12866-2288. (518) 587-8770,
> www.humorproject.com

The American Association of Therapeutic Humor

Newsletters, resources and conferences dealing with therapeutic uses of humor are available. Check out their web site at www.AATH.org.

The World Laughter Tour, Inc.

United States Laughter Clubs,
1159 South Creekway Court, Gahanna, Ohio 43230
www.worldlaughtertour.com

RECOMMENDED READING

Humor and Humor Related

Blumenfeld, Esther and Lynne Alpern. *Humor at Work*. Atlanta, GA: Peachtree Publishers, 1994.

Cousins, Norman. *Anatomy of an Illness*. New York: W.W. Norton, 1979.

Freiberg, Kevin and Jackie. *Nuts! Southwest Airlines' Crazy Recipe for Business and Personal Success*. Austin, TX: Bard Press, 1996.

Garland, Ron. *Making Work Fun*. San Diego, CA: Shamrock Press, 1991.

Goodman, Joel. *Laffirmations: 1,001 Ways to Add Humor to Your Life and Work*. Deerfield Beach, FL: Health Communications Inc., 1995.

Hemsath, Dave, and Leslie Yerkes. *301 Ways to Have Fun at Work*. San Francisco, CA: Berrett-Koehler Publishers, Inc., 1997.

Jenkins, Ron. *Subversive Laughter*. New York: The Free Press, 1994.

Kataria, Dr. Madan. *Laugh For No Reason*. 1999. (You can special order this book about the Laughter Club phenomenon at www.worldlaughtertour.com)

Klein, Allen. *The Courage to Laugh*. New York: Jeremy P. Tarcher/Putnam, 1998.

Klein, Allen. *The Healing Power of Humor*. New York: Jeremy P. Tarcher/Putnam, 1989.

Metcalf, C.W., and Roma Felible. *Lighten Up*. Reading, MA: Addison-Wesley, 1992.

Mikes, George. *Humor in Memoriam*. London: Routledge & Kegan Paul, 1970.

Morreall, John. *Humor Works*. Amherst, MA: HRD Press, Inc., 1997.

Morreall, John. *Taking Laughter Seriously*. Albany, NY: State University of New York Press, 1983.

Robinson, Vera M. *Humor and the Health Professions*. Thorofare, NJ: Slack Incorporated, 1991.

Seaward, Brian Luke. *Stressed is Desserts Spelled Backwards*. Berkley, CA: Conari Press, 1999.

Weinstein, Matt. *Managing to Have Fun*. New York: Fireside, 1996.

Wooten, Patty. *Compassionate Laughter*. Salt Lake City, UT: Commune-A-Key, 1996.

Creativity

Adams, James L. *Conceptual Blockbusting*. Reading, MA: Addison-Wesley, 1974.

De Bono, Edward. *Serious Creativity*. New York: HarperCollins, 1992.

De Bono, *Six Action Shoes*. New York: Harper Business, 1991.

Fobes, Richard. *The Creative Problem Solver's Toolbox*. Corvallis, OR: Solutions Through Innovation, 1993.

Hall, Doug. *Jump Start Your Brain*. New York: Warner Books, 1995.

Oech, Roger von. *A Whack on the Side of the Head*. Stamford, CT: U.S. Games Systems Inc., 1983.

Ray, Michael, and Rochelle Myers. *Creativity in Business*. New York: Doubleday, 1986.

Robinson, Alan G., and Sam Stern. *Corporate Creativity*. San Francisco, CA: Berret-Koehler Publishers, Inc., 1997.

Thompson, Charles "Chic." *What a Great Idea!* New York: Harper Perennial, 1992.

Vangundy, Arthur B. *Brain Boosters for Business Advantage*. San Diego, CA: Pfeiffer & Company, 1995.

Wujec, Tom. *Five Star Mind*. New York: Doubleday, 1995.

Wycoff, Joyce. *Mindmapping*. New York: Berkeley Books, 1986.

Miscellaneous

Anderson, Kristin, and Ron Zemke. *Delivering Knock Your Socks Off Service*. New York: American Management Association, 1991.

Csikszentmihalyi, Mihaly. *Flow—The Psychology of Optimal Experience*. New York: Harper Perennial, 1990.

Frankl, Viktor. *Man's Search for Meaning*. New York: Simon and Schuster, 1963.

Glanz, Barbara A. *Care Packages for the Workplace*. New York: McGraw-Hill, 1996.

Gross, T. Scott. *Positively Outrageous Customer Service*. New York: Mastermedia Limited, 1991.

Kriegel, Robert, and David Brandt. *Sacred Cows Make the Best Burgers*. New York: Warner Books, 1996.

Nelson, Bob. *1,001 Ways to Energize Employees*. New York: Workman Publishing, 1997.

Nelson, Bob. *1,001 Ways to Reward Your Employees*. New York: Workman Publishing, 1994.

Posen, David B. *Staying Afloat When the Water Gets Rough*. Toronto, ON: Key Porter Books, 1998.

You Can't Be Serious! Putting Humor to Work
KEYNOTE TALKS AND WORKSHOPS WITH MICHAEL KERR

You Can't Be Serious! keynotes and workshops are fast-paced, humor-filled and full of practical tips on how audiences can boost their humor quotient in the workplace. Presentations are customized to suit your particular audience's needs or conference theme. The programs include door prizes (Humor First Aid Kits), fun takeaways and resource handouts for all the participants.

Choose from one of the following eight program themes . . .

You Can't Be Serious! – Putting Humor to Work
Laugh for the Health of It – Humor as a Stress Buster
Managing to Have Fun – Humor Skills for Supervisors and Managers
Humor Me – Energize Your Presentations With Humor
Customer Service With a Laugh
Mastering Change With Humor
We Have to Stop Meeting Like This! – Energize Your Meetings With Humor
From Ha Ha to AHA! – The Creativity and Humor Dynamic Duo

YOUR PRESENTER . . . MICHAEL KERR

Michael Kerr is a dynamic international speaker. Michael combines his "serious" background as a communications manager with his "not-so-serious" background as a humorist, humor author and theater improviser to provide a unique perspective on the role of humor in our work lives. His programs are based on more than 10 years of research into applied humor and organizational behavior. Michael is a certified *Laughter Leader* for the World Laughter Tour and a member of the American Association of Therapeutic Humor and the International Group for Humor Studies. Michael writes a regular humor column for *Home Business Report* magazine and is also the author of *When Do You Let the Animals Out? A Field Guide to Rocky Mountain Humour* and *The Canadian Rockies Guide to Wildlife Watching*.

For more information on how to book a program or to order more books contact:
Michael Kerr: 322 Canyon Close, Canmore, Alberta, Canada, T1W 1H4
Telephone: (403) 609-2640 Toll free (Canada and the U.S.)1-866-609-2640
mkerr@banff.net   www.mikekerr.com